330.1
P87e

116704

DATE DUE			
Oct 2 '81			

The Economic Value of
the Quality of Life

Other Titles in This Series

Also of Interest

Westview Special Studies in Contemporary Social Issues

The Economic Value of
the Quality of Life
Thomas M. Power

Disputing the casting of the environmental debate of the 1970s as a conflict between economic and environmental or social values, Professor Power asserts that environmental values are no less "economic" than the values of commodities sold on the market. The resources of the physical and social environment--measured as "quality of life" (QOL)--and the services they provide contribute to human well-being in exactly the same way as marketable natural or human-made resources, and in that sense enter into the determination of human economic well-being in an identical way.

Professor Power analyzes wage differentials between areas that have different QOLs and studies particular environmental services, such as security against violent crime, high quality recreational opportunities, clean air, and congestion, to demonstrate quantitatively their value in determining economic welfare. The book closes with the suggestion that much of the discussion of regional economic well-being is both mistaken and misleading: per capita money income is not a good measure of economic well-being, and economic growth and growth in economic welfare may not be closely linked.

Thomas M. Power is professor and chairman of the Economics Department, University of Montana.

The Economic Value of
the Quality of Life

Thomas M. Power

Westview Press / Boulder, Colorado

*Westview Special Studies in
Contemporary Social Issues*

Published in 1980 in the United States of America by
      Westview Press, Inc.
      5500 Central Avenue
      Boulder, Colorado 80301
      Frederick A. Praeger, Publisher

Library of Congress Catalog Card Number: 80-10873
ISBN: 0-89158-869-8

Composition for this book was provided by the author.
Printed and bound in the United States of America.

*To a woman who has demonstrated for her
family that through love, care, and hard
work, a very high quality of life can be
created even in a deteriorating metropolis,
my mother*

Edith Thomas Power

this book is gratefully dedicated.

Contents

Tables

Acknowledgments

This book grew out of research funded by the Montana Department of Labor and Industry. As part of Montana Governor Thomas Judge's "Montana Futures Project," the Department funded a sweeping analysis of all parts of the Montana economy. Dr. Richard Bourke, director of the project, asked me to look at a part of Montana which was not usually treated "economically," namely the quality of life in Montana, and analyze ways in which consideration of the quality of life could enter into decision making influencing the economic future of Montana. The basic arguments of the book emerged as a result of that analysis.

Much of the book was written while on extended backpacking trips in the Selway-Bitterroot Wilderness. For that reason I would like to thank my children for patiently putting up with such perverse behavior on my part on our vacations. I would also like to express my appreciation to the architects of the National Wilderness System who had the foresight to set aside wild natural areas such as the Selway-Bitterroot.

Professor Richard Barrett played the critical role of devil's advocate in challenging most of my arguments and deflating some of the pretensions. In addition he helped considerably with the organization. Professor John Duffield made several crucial suggestions which tightened up the argument and also was the one who urged to me seek a wider audience through publication.

Kathy Mrgudic deciphered my scribblings and translated them quickly and with good humor into the several drafts which evolved into this book. She lightened considerably the gruesome task of editing the manuscript.

Although all of the above and others must be held responsible for not convincing me of the errors of my ways and setting me "straight," given my Irish stubbornness, they must be excused from the remaining confusion and errors.

Thomas M. Power

1
Economics and the Quality of Life

1. INTRODUCTION

Throughout the 1970s the debate over environmental protection has pitted the "preservationist" against the "economic
developer." The dialogue has been conducted in terms which
seem to have been mutually agreed upon by both factions.
Those terms conveniently distinguish between "economic" values
and "environmental" or "social" values. The pursuit of economic values brings with it changes in the physical and social
environment which threaten the "environmental" or "social"
values. There is, we are told in the economist's jargon, a
trade-off between the two. Further improvement in economic
well being often can be purchased only at the expense of a
deterioration in the "quality of life."

Almost any discussion of environmental or economic development issues is cast in these terms. All participants in
the debate pay at least lip-service respect to the reality and
importance both of the "quality of life" and the need for further economic development. As far back as 1970 when a Presidential Commission was brooding over "national goals," its
staff gave official recognition to this "new" value: "At the
beginning of the seventies a seemingly new aspect has been
added to the list of national goals. The search for 'quality
of life' and the appeal for reordering the national priorities
embody the essense of this new aspect."*

What was "new" was the emergence of this concern in con-
trast to the over-riding national commitment ever since the
end of World War II to the growth of jobs and incomes.

Cast in these terms, the debate over environmental protection often degenerates into a debate between allegedly

---

*Cited in Lowdon Wingo, "The Quality of Life: Toward a Micro-
economic Definition." Urban Studies 10 (1973): 3.

hard-nosed practical individuals who see the need for additional output of commodities, the expansion of job opportunities,
and a rise in the real level of income especially for the
poor on the one side and "idealists" who wish to pursue the
lost environmental innocence of the past on the other side.
The latter are often seen as pursuing spiritual values in con-
trast to the material values of the former. The preservation-
ists' language is heavily moral and sociological. The de-
velopers' is concrete and practical. Concepts like the "quality of life" are used by both sides in a way that suggests
that they are vague sociological or moral incantations designed more to invoke a (hopefully) shared set of social values and assert a moral superiority than to convey information
or make a logical point.

This study will argue that the distinction discussed
above between "economic values" and "social values" such as the
"quality of life" is a misleading and dangerous distinction.
There is nothing especially ethereal or spiritual or "non-
economic" about the quality of life (QOL). Similarly there is
nothing especially "material," practical," or "economic" about
job opportunities or money prices.

Economics, as a social science, does not focus particular
attention on the material as opposed to the spiritual. It
does not accept money values as somehow more important or basic than human values. It does not respect market activity
as more crucial or fundamental than household or "leisure"
activity. Economists, in pursuing income opportunities for
themselves may have leaned in a particular direction. Economists as empirical scientists may have been led by the abun-
dance of a particular type of easily organized empirical evidence to focus their attention disproportionately on particular issues. But economics as a science is not and should not
be limited by these very human biases of its practitioners.

Economists take as part of their basic data human values.
It is with reference to those human values that economists
discuss the rationality with which our limited resources get
used. Economists do not divide those values into material and
spiritual, practical and ideal, market and non-market, etc.
and choose to focus on only some selected human values. Economists only make one distinction, a behavioral distinction:
they focus on values which *affect the way people behave in
their use of scarce resources.* Clearly the spiritual values of
an esthete monk as well as the spiritual values of the Pha-
raohes and medieval bishops affected the pattern of resource
use no less than the material values of merchants and manu-
facturers. Also the resources referred to are not necessarily
material. Human effort, initiative, and entrepreneurship, in
short - human motivation, is probably the most crucial of all
resources and certainly is as much mental and cultural as material. Similarly, social environments with particular characteristics and particular esthetic aspects of the physical

environment are scarce resources which individuals pursue but
are not usually labeled "material."

Economics as a science encompasses the analysis of the
interaction of *all* human values which affect human behavior
towards scarce resources and the pattern of use of *any* resource which is scarce.

Thus the QOL is as much an economic concept as it is a
sociological or spiritual concept. The QOL is *not* a vague
etherial concept of concern only to a minority of environmental purists or rich dilettantes or ivory tower philosophers.
It encompasses very valuable services rendered to all citizens
daily by the physical and social environment. To ignore the
QOL or dismiss it, is to threaten these valuable services with
loss or degradation. Millions of citizens regularly modify
their activities in pursuit of these valuable services. Because of this, QOL is amenable to social science analysis. In
particular, an economic analysis of individuals' behavior in
pursuit of a higher QOL opens up the possibility of quantitatively estimating the value these individuals place on particular "qualities of life."

This study is a preliminary exploration of this possibility. As such it should be considered a first tentative step
intended to provoke thought, debate, and further analysis. It
makes no pretense at being conclusive or thorough. It does
attempt to be rigorous in its logic and honest in its pursuit
of the elusive truth about the character of our citizens' economic and socioeconomic well-being.

2. DEFINING THE "QUALITY OF LIFE"

Following Wingo,[*] we define the "quality of life " as the
quality of the social and physical (both human-made and natural) environment in which people pursue the gratification of
their wants and needs. The QOL encompasses the character of
the external experiential environments in which people live
their lives. It provides the backdrop against which all human
activity takes place and provides a flow of valuable services
to people which make their "pursuit of happiness" both possible and easier. There is nothing mysterious or ethereal a-
bout the QOL. Social, human-made, and natural environments
which allow people to live comfortable, healthy, productive,
and secure lives are in limited supply and unevenly distributed. As a result people privately and collectively must expend part of their limited resources to attain them. Significant amounts of human activity are devoted to attaining or improving the QOL. People save part of their regular income to

---

[*] Wingo, "The Quality of Life: Toward a Microeconomic Definition," op. cit.

purchase housing which provides the most immediate human-made environment upon which they depend. The housing decision also involves a locational decision which involves choice among a variety of natural and social environments and the commitment of resources to migration. The social environment is heavily dependent upon collective, political activity which involves a substantial commitment of time and resources by some and the approval by the majority of taxation and government expenditures aimed at improving the social and physical environment of settled areas. In pursuing a higher QOL people both individually and collectively trade one limited resource for another. Travel time and expense (leisure time and income) are exchanged for more homogeneous, pleasant, and secure neighborhoods. A less congested and more manageable small town or rural environment are exchanged for higher pay and a more polluted and less secure life in a large city. Private income and individual control are traded through government taxation and regulation for a more managed social environment. Individuals make investments in themselves and their children which develop their ability to enjoy more fully certain aspects of their external environments and which, therefore, make those aspects of their environment more valuable to them.

Because the experiential environments upon which the QOL depends are in limited supply, because the services with which they provide people are valuable, and because people individually and/or collectively expend other limited resources in pursuing them, the QOL has a significant aspect that is amenable to economic analysis. For economic analysis focuses exactly on the relative values implicit in such tradeoffs between scarce resources in the pursuit of human objectives. This paper will attempt to use the tools of economic analysis to establish the relative value of the QOL which the natural, human-made, and social environments of any area provides its residents. It will study the way people have, in fact, behaved, the structured choices they have made about the environments in which they live, and try to infer from this how they value these external environments.

3. MONEY INCOME AND ECONOMIC WELFARE

Economic analysis in the past has implicitly suggested that the QOL was primarily determined by the quantity and range of commodities (private, tradeable, reproducible goods and services) available to the population. Thus the welfare of the population was defined and discussed in terms of the total productive capacity of the economy or the average or median share of that output available to the population. Gross national product (GNP) and per capita income were the primary measures of that welfare. In today's context this seems strangely narrow, for these are largely measures of output, not consumption, and ignore some of the most obvious components of welfare like leisure time or the effort necessary to attain a particular level of material well-being, as well as the QOL.

This narrow focus of economic analysis can be explained in two ways. First, leisure and the QOL may be goods which become valuable only after certain basic needs are satisfied. Thus, when basic shelter, food, and clothing could not be provided with certainty, people were willing to work 16 hour days in heavily polluted and congested environments. As the quantity and quality of these basic material goods available grew, the value of additional units declined relative to the value of leisure and other non-marketed goods and services. As more and more of the physical and social environment was sacrificed to production activities, the more valuable the remaining high quality environments became. Thus a natural relative shift in emphasis took place from commodities to other valuable, but non-marketed, goods and services. The current public concern with the QOL reflects this shift.

The other explanation for the past (and present) narrow emphasis of economics is more critical of the vision and ideological bias of this social science and its practitioners. Much of the history of Anglo-American economics has consisted of the attempt to prove that a market economy built around individual ownership of productive resources and the private pursuit of private gain would result in a socially optional pattern of resource use. Rebelling against the arbitrary and autocractic control by government and church over productive human activity characteristic of the federal and mercantilist periods, economics attempted to show that a society made up of individual "shop keepers" pursuing their own interests, unregulated by anything but the demands of a competitive market, would be both prosperous and socially rational.

In making this case, economists focused on goods and services which the market handled best: those which were divisible, from which non-purchasers could be easily excluded, and which had prices which accurately reflected the cost associated with their production. Economics, in short, focused on tradeable commodities. In addition, economics assumed the simplest of social situations: one in which a person's production or consumption activities had no impact on any other person that was not accounted for by the market. Unfortunately there are valuable goods and services which are crucial to individual welfare which do not have these commodity features, and in a built-up urban area, there are few production or consumption activities that have no "spillover" effects on others. As a result, the basic assumptions of traditional economics fail. Since some valuable things never become commodities because individuals cannot be easily excluded from using them, no price comes to be attached to them and the market fails to adequately account for their production and/or use. Similarly, the spillover effects of one person's activity on another's welfare gets ignored. In short, the market fails and if people wish to rationally produce and/or use these goods and services and regulate the impact they have on each other, they must act collectively, that is, socially and/or politically. Government, which economics originally sought to relegate to a minor role in economic activity, becomes, potentially, a necessary economic participant again. Anglo-American economics and economists have sought to avoid this conclusion for over two centuries and in the process have ignored some of the fundamental aspects of economic welfare. The QOL encompasses many of them. For because the QOL, as we have defined it, focuses on the character of the physical and social environment, it has many of the features of a non-traded or non-tradeable good described above. Given our legal system which allows free migration, individuals cannot be easily excluded from making use of a particular natural or social environment. Given that the use of these environments by increasing numbers of people, after some point, causes the degradation of those environments, the spillover effects of individuals' private activities are important in determining the QOL. Thus the QOL has not easily fitted into the market and commodity-oriented economics of the past and as a result has been ignored or defined primarily in terms of commodities. Economic theory, however, over the last two decades has taken tentative steps towards correcting this narrow and misleading focus. This paper attempts to continue in that direction by insisting that the QOL which any citizen enjoys or suffers with is as crucial an element in their well-being as the money income they receive. This is not offered as an individual opinion about what is good or valuable for Americans but as a statement about how Americans themselves have, in fact, valued their physical and social environment. That valuation is implicit in their observable actions and choices.

4.   THE ECONOMIST'S BEHAVIORAL ANALYSIS OF HUMAN VALUES

In trying to establish the value which people place on such non-marketed goods and services as those which establish the quality of life in a particular area, economists tend to be very skeptical of direct interview techniques. Rather than depending upon what people *say* something is worth, economists study the actual behavior of people. Working from the assumption that people rationally pursue what they judge to be best for themselves, economists try to infer from the behavior of large numbers of people the relative values implicit in that behavior. "Talk" is looked upon as "cheap" when compared to the real resources individuals have to commit when they follow one path of behavior rather than another. Thus economists tend to trust the analysis of behavior more than the analysis of interview results.

Two quite different approaches will be taken in this study

to estimate the value of a particular area's QOL relative to
other areas in the United States. The first will be indirect
and aggregate: wage differentials will be studied to approxi-
mate the net value of a particular area's QOL compared with
the national average. It is on this that the following three
chapters will focus.

Chapter 5 will then take another approach looking at particular aspects of the social and physical environment and
trying to directly estimate the value of an area's advantage
in each of the aspects studied relative to the nation as a
whole. In this approach, individual's behavior is again used
to establish the value associated with each advantage a particular area has.

5. THE ADEQUACY OF THE ECONOMIST'S APPROACH TO VALUE

Given the past emphasis of both economists and economics
on commodity production and exchange in the commercial market
place, many will be surprised by the assertions that economic
analysis need not and should not be limited to these "commercial" values. Others will be suspicious as to just what economists are driving at when they talk of value and values.
To some, this is the domain of philosophy, psychology, and
ethics. Others may interpret the economists' assertions about
the "value" of the quality of life as economists telling
people how they ought to value the QOL or as personal evaluations by economists which are being foisted off on the general population.

Rather than discuss these problems in the abstract, we
will proceed to apply the tools of economic analysis to the
problem of the value of the quality of life and return to
these questions in Chapter 6 where the meaning of "value" and
the limits of conventional economic analysis will be more fully explored.

2
Interpreting Wage Differentials as Measures of Differentially Valued Qualities of Life

1. INTRODUCTION

In this Chapter we informally introduce the idea of using wage differentials to measure the way in which individuals in fact value the QOL in different areas. In the next chapter a more formal, mathematical approach is taken. The chapter following that presents the empirical evidence and, as an example, applies it to a particular state.

2. THE THEORY OF COMPENSATING WAGE DIFFERENTIALS: A VERBAL INTRODUCTION

If certain areas do in fact have superior social and physical environments, people will, over time, "vote with their feet" and tend to move to those areas or tend not to move away from such areas. If other areas have congested, impersonal, and crime-ridden social environments and heavily polluted and ugly physical environments, people will tend to avoid these areas: they will not move there unless other advantages outweigh these negative features and will move away whenever opportunities present themselves. The net effect of this behavior over time will be that in the areas with an attractive QOL there will be a relatively larger supply of labor and in those with degraded QOL a relatively restricted supply of labor. Business firms seeking to operate in the degraded areas will find that they have to pay relatively high wages if they are to get and hold workers, while firms operating in the regions with an attractive QOL will find that they can pay relatively lower wages and still obtain a work force.

In a competitive economy, firms in the degraded area will not be able to pay relatively higher wages and stay competitive with firms in other areas unless they derive some special advantage from being located in the degraded area. The economic explanations for the growth of urban areas in particular locations have focused on just such locational advantages to

firms: lower transportation costs in both obtaining raw materials and distributing final products, the economic advantages
of specializiation which go with large urban areas, etc. Thus
relatively higher wages will be paid in an area if it has two
characteristics: it has disadvantages for workers which they
seek to avoid and it has advantages to some firms which seek
to locate there. Only if *both* conditions are met will wages
in such an area rise relative to other areas. If workers have
no preferences which draw them away from the area, profit maximizing firms will not pay them higher wages even if the firms,
because they derive economic advantages from the location,
could "afford" to pay higher wages. Instead the economic value of the locational advantage will be passed on to the owners of fixed resources in the area, especially to landowners
as "economic rent," and wages will be the same as elsewhere.
Similarly, if an area has no locational advantages to firms
but is unattractive to workers, no wage differential will develop for a competitive firm could not afford to pay higher
wages. Firms simply will not locate there, nor will workers.

In discussing the number of people actually working in a
particular area and the relative wage rates paid, economists
divide the determinants into two categories: those affecting
people's willingness to work (supply of labor) and those affecting business firms' willingness to hire workers (demand
for labor). The above discussion points out that for differences in wages to develop between regions, *both* supply factors
(workers' dislike for an area) *and* demand factors (firms' ability to pay higher wages) must operate.

Economic theory and empirical analysis has established
that some firms do derive economic advantage from certain
areas. This is usually used to explain the development of
large urban areas. The increased concern with the quality of
life suggests that certain areas because of their inferior
physical and social environment are also less desirable locations for people to live. Thus we may have the supply and demand conditions necessary for wage differentials to develop,
and it may be possible to use these wage differentials to establish the differential value individuals place on the QOL
in one area as opposed to another.

Put in its simplest form, the interpretation of these
wage differentials will be the following: in a competitive
economy with a fairly mobile labor force, workers and their
families will have to be fully compensated for any disadvantage
an area has before they will choose to locate there. Workers
will look at the total real "income" they will receive as a
result of locating in any particular area. This income will
be determined by the money wages they get paid, the money cost
of living in the particular area, and the non-marketed goods
and services with which the social and physical environment
provides them. As long as certain areas because of superior
environmental values, superior government services, superior

wages, or lower costs of living, have relative advantages, workers will relocate to those areas. Migration will continue until there is no further reason for further migration, until the total real income or net welfare of workers is the same in all areas. In this equilibrium situation differential money wages will have to have exactly compensated individuals for the disadvantages of living in certain areas. If the wage levels are not high enough to completely compensate workers, outmigration will continue. If the wage levels more than compensate, inmigration will continue. At equilibrium we can interpret the wage differentials as full money payment for the disadvantages (or advantages) of living in a particular area. Those wage differentials tell us the value workers "voting with their feet" place on the differences in the QOL among areas.

The general result described above follows from a conclusion very familiar to economists: in a competitive economy with reasonably mobile resources, resources will move until an equilibrium is reached in which there is no advantage to be obtained from further movement of resources. This would suggest that in general no area within a national economy can obtain a net advantage over others unless it can restrict the inflow of migrants seeking to share in that regional advantage. Thus any particular area from the point of view of the welfare of its residents, cannot, in an economy which does allow free labor mobility, be very much worse off or better off than other areas.* This should not be interpreted to mean that it does not matter what happens to an area's environment. By itself degradation of environmental resources which reduces the value of the services flowing from them makes both the local population and the nation as a whole worse off.

If we wish, then, to place a value on the assumed higher QOL in a particular area, we need only look at the wage differentials between that area and the national average or that area and the nation's large urban areas. This places an objectively determined, quantitative, dollar value on the area's QOL *advantage* vis-à-vis the rest of the nation or any particular area in the nation. To some this will be a startling result: an area's *lower* wages are a measure not of the disadvantages of living there but of the environmental (social and physical) advantages of living there. What has been often pointed to as a measure, for instance, of small towns' and rural areas' failure to keep up with the rest of the nation economically is really a measure of their success in not having their social and physical environments degraded as rapidly

---

*This conclusion makes several assumptions about the mobility of labor and costs associated with the mobility of labor which will be discussed below.

as those elsewhere. Because this may seem to be a counter-
intuitive result involving logical "trickery," we will submit
it to careful logical and empirical analysis before actually
interpreting the data in this way. In the next chapter, we
develop the argument in traditional theoretical terms and discuss the statistical problems associated with estimating the
appropriate wage differentials. In this chapter we consider
the alternative explanations which could be given for the wage
differentials which exist between areas.

3. COMPENSATING WAGE DIFFERENTIALS AND
   THE OPTIMAL QUALITY OF ENVIRONMENTAL RESOURCES

Since Tiebout*, economists have suggested that the existence of regions and cities with different QOL, cost of living,
taxes, government services, etc., combined with free migration
of the population to preferred areas allowed a market mimick-
ing adjustment process which would allow individuals to "vote
with their feet" and choose utility maximizing combinations of
those local characteristics. For instance, those living in
polluted areas would get compensated by being paid higher
wages and thus there would be no "social cost" associated with
pollution.** Both intuitive reflection and mathematical modeling demonstrates that this conclusion is not correct. Individuals, in choosing where to live, look only at the level of
money wages, cost of living, and QOL they will obtain. However, their relocation will affect the QOL of the individual
communities both into which they move and out of which they
move. For instance, a person choosing to move into a congested city to accept the higher wages paid there will increase
the congestion costs all residents have to bear. The individual will ignore these spillover or external impacts. In economists' jargon, this is a typical "pure public good" problem.
The result of these individual decisions will be "too much"
migration to certain areas and "too much" congestion from a
social optimal (Pareto) point of view. Polinsky and Rubinfeld
hint at this in suggesting that the external effects of location decisions on density have to be taken into account in any
general equilibrium analysis of migration and location.***

---

*Charles M. Tiebout, "The Pure Theory of Local Government Ex-
penditures," Journal of Political Economy, 64 (1956):416-424.

**Irving Hoch, "City Size Effects," op. cit., pp. 861-862.

***A. Mitchell Polinsky and Daniel L. Rubinfeld, "The Long-Run
Effects of a Residential Property Tax and Local Public Services," Journal of Urban Economics 5 (1978): 241-262.

Seskin analyzes exactly this problem in a general equilibrium context.* Thus the analysis in this paper of compensating wage differentials is not to be interpreted as suggesting that wage adjustments fully compensate the population for degrada- tion of the QOL nor that the resulting "free market" solution is optimal. Degradation of the QOL leaves the population, on net, worse off because a valuable resource has been lost. Mi- gration and the resulting compensating wage variations do not eliminate this loss, they merely distribute it to the nation's entire population.

4. QOL AND POPULATION SIZE

In order to be able to analyze the way wage differentials vary from area to area and relate this to the quality of life, we draw on a well-established body of empirical evidence on wage differentials. This literature analyzes the way wages vary with city size. Victor Fuchs, in a National Bureau of Economic Research monograph,** has demonstrated that there are large and persistent differences in wage earnings between cities of different sizes even after the data is adjusted for labor quality, region, and occupation.

These wage differentials between cities of different size are easily understood in terms of the need for compensa- tion for living in less attractive areas. The attractiveness of a city to a worker may vary with the size for several rea- sons:

A. The Cost of Living Will Be Higher

i. As cities grow, centrally located land increases in value and rents rise thus housing costs will be higher. Such higher rents can be avoided by living further from the econo- mic center, but then transportation costs will be higher.

ii. The price of locally purchased goods and services will be higher because both rents and labor costs are higher and these will be passed on to consumers.

iii. There may be diseconomies of scale in providing some government services such as traffic and crime control. Thus there will be higher taxes unassociated with improved govern- ment services.

---

*Eugene P. Seskin, "Residential Choice and Air Pollution: A General Equilibrium Model," American Economic Review 63, no. 5 (December 1973): 960-967.

**Differentials in Hourly Earnings by Region and City Size, 1959. Occasional Paper 101, 1961, Columbia Univ. Press.

iv. There are money costs associated with the lower quality of life which goes with city size which are discussed below: higher health, cleaning, and maintenance costs associated
with air pollution; higher insurance premiums and private
crime control costs associated with higher crime rates, etc.

B. The Quality of the Physical and Social
   Environment Will Be Lower.

   i. Congestion, besides adding to rents and transportation
costs, adds to the length of time it takes to get to work,
stores, recreation, etc. It also adds to the frustration associated with high density traffic and traffic jams.

   ii. Air pollution and water pollution increase with city
size. Although, as demonstrated by Montana's cities, pollution
problems are not limited to large cities, the severity of them
does increase with city size.*

   iii. Crime rates increase dramatically with city size.
This is just one of the more dramatic forms of social breakdown which accompanies growth in city size. This will be
discussed and documented below.

   Given these welfare losses which increase with city size,
it is not surprising that workers in larger cities have to be
paid more to get them to live and work there. But it is important to know whether these higher wages are one of the advantages of living in larger urban areas or are merely compensation for the real welfare costs associated with living in
such areas. The following section investigates explanations
for these wage differentials which do not involve QOL or cost
of living (COL) differences.

5. ALTERNATIVE EXPLANATIONS OF WAGE DIFFERENTIALS

   Economic theory and the economics literature offer several explanations for wage differentials other than the "compensation payments" explanation offered above. Here we review those other explanations.

   This consideration of all possible alternative explanations is necessary because the value of the quality of life,
like many other important economic concepts such as technological improvement, human capital, and changes in product quality, cannot be measured directly. It is a residual which

---

*Irving Hoch, "City Size Effects, Trends, and Policies,
Science 193, September 3, 1976, p. 859.

remains after all market determined impacts on well-being have
been accounted for. It is tied to human economic activities
which cannot be explained by these other market-based forces.
Thus "proof" of its existence and size proceeds by showing
that other, more direct and conventional, approaches cannot
explain the phenomenon while the proffered concept, in this
case the QOL, can. The "proof" is a process of elimination
combined with persuasive, but untestable argument as to the
"intuitive appeal" of the explanation offered. This approach
is somewhat frustrating because it seems to "beat around the
bush" by dragging in one possible argument after another only
to reject it as in conflict with existing data. Then, after
this exhaustive (and exhausting) process, it declares the original, untestable hypothesis, to be the sole survivor and,
therefore, the "most likely" explanation. But the nature of
our problem, the evaluation of a set of diverse, non-marketed
environmental services, forces this approach upon us. Much of
economic theory has a very similar nature; it involves primarily the identification and "naming" of residuals or residual
behavior which conventional theory up to that point had not
been able to explain. The alternative to this approach as applied to the value of the quality of life is the more direct
but less complete and piecemeal, approach taken in Chapter 5.

A. Disequilibrium in the Labor Market

The most common explanation for wage differentials is
tied to surplus labor accumulating in a particular area. If
economic and technological change cause the demand for labor
in a particular area to decline or to not increase as fast as
the natural growth in the population, competition for jobs in
that area will cause wages to decline. If part of the work
force is mobile, these falling wages will encourage outmigration and discourage inmigration so that in the long run the
differentials should disappear as labor supply (and, with the
relocation of some industry to low wage areas , labor demand)
adjust. The wage differentials are temporary phenomena which
serve the economic function of adjusting labor markets to a
new equilibrium. If technological and economic change have
affected rural areas and small cities more than large cities
and if this change has been ongoing so that continuous adjustment was necessary, one would expect to see the sort of wage
differentials by city size described above: lower wages in
smaller cities and rural areas.
Although this explanation has considerable intuitive appeal, migration patterns over the last decade and a half do
not support it. This explanation suggests that the wage differentials are necessary to encourage the relocation of the
labor force from low-wage areas to high-wage areas. However,
if one looks at the population growth rates between 1960 and
1970 (see Table 2.1), one does not find any such systematic

Table 2.1

GROWTH IN POPULATION 1960-70, FOR SMSA's BY
REGION AND POPULATION CLASS, 1960

Class	Population Size in 000, 1960	All	Per cent Growth of SMSA's in Class, 1960-70			
			North-east	North Central	South	West
1	Below 250	16%	10	13	13	39
2	250-500	13%	7	12	15	18
3	500-1,000	23%	11	12	20	44
4	1,000-2,000	18%	8	12	29	27
5	2,000 +	11%	6	11	38	16

Source: 1970 Census of Population, reported in Irving Hoch,
"Income and City Size," Urban Studies 9 (1972): 312.

relationship. Similarly, if one looks at population growth rates during the first half of this decade, one finds that smaller places (*lower* wage areas) were growing at a considerably faster rate than larger cities. Regression analysis which takes into account regional differences, the decline in the aerospace industry, growth in centers of government activity, and the growth of areas adjacent to the "Standard Metropolitan Statistical Areas" (SMSA) indicates that the smaller the city, the faster has been the rate of growth of population and the higher the net inmigration rate (see Table 2.2). Thus low-wage areas are gaining in population relative to high-wage areas, the opposite of what one would expect from the "disequilibrium" theory. People are migrating to and not moving away from the low-wage areas.

If one looks at the wage differential between cities of different sizes over time, one finds that it has narrowed considerably between 1929 and 1950 but has been stable since then.* This suggests that although labor market disequilibrium caused larger wage differentials by city size in the past, labor market adjustments by 1950 had eliminated that part caused by excess supply and the remaining differentials are tied to other causes such as compensation payments.

B. Different Industry Mix

Some observers have suggested that the higher wages paid in large cities are due to the presence there of "high wage" industries.** If industries which employ more capital per worker tend to locate in larger cities, and these industries pay higher wages, then one would find differences in wages which are "explained" by differences in industry-mix. The problem with this explanation is that it ignores the supply side of the problem and focuses only on demand. Firms which can "afford to pay" higher wages are assumed to pay those higher wages. But profit maximizing firms will do no such thing unless they have to in order to obtain their work force. That is, they will not pay higher wages unless something restricts the labor supply that is available where they are located. Thus we need to explain why labor is not available in the large urban areas before we have explained anything. This carries us back to our original problem. As Goldfarb and Yezer put it:

---

*Irving Hoch, "Income and City Size," Urban Studies 9, no. 3 (October 1972): 314-315.

**See for instance, Paul E. Polzin, "State and Regional Wage Differentials," Southern Economic Journal (January 1972): 371-378.

Table 2.2

REGRESSION EQUATIONS EXPLAINING RECENT POPULATION
CHANGES IN METROPOLITAN AREAS (SMSA's)

Independent variables**	1974 as percent of 1970	1974 as percent of 1973	1973 as percent of 1970	Migration as percent of 1970
	Coefficients			
Constant (base change)	102.07	100.14	101.93	-0.92
SMSA population, 1970 (in millions)	-0.77*	-0.17*	-0.60*	-0.60*
South	2.51*	0.81*	1.67*	1.29
West	4.30*	1.61*	2.59*	3.81*
Sunny West***	8.24*	0.91*	7.10*	6.91*
Alaska	11.45*	0.33	10.90*	6.20
Florida	15.80*	3.63*	11.32*	17.80*
Texas	3.05*	0.81*	2.13*	2.01
West Virginia	-5.54*	-1.49*	-3.97*	-3.46
Capitals, inc. D.C.	2.90*	0.47	2.39*	2.64*
Aerospace areas	-13.54*	-2.18*	-10.89*	-13.77*
New SMSA's	3.28*	0.38	2.76*	3.61*
	$\bar{R}^2$'s			
Explained variance	0.55	0.44	0.55	0.55

*Significant at the 0.05 level.

**All variables except SMSA population are discrete variables with values of 1 (for appearance) or 0 (for non-appearance) in the relation. A particular SMSA can take on a value of 1 in a number of such variables, for example. Melbourne-Titusville-Cocoa is in the South, in Florida, in Aerospace areas and in new SMSA's.

***Includes SMSA's in Arizona, Colorado, Nevada, New Mexico, Utah, Hawaii, and California, except San Francisco, Los Angeles, and SMSA's in the Central Valley.

Source: Irving Hoch, "City Size Effects, Trends, and Policies," Science 143 (September 3, 1976), p. 861.

"...there are no inherently high wage industries--only firms choosing to locate in high wage areas due to locational advantages."* We have to explain what it is that makes some areas "high wage" areas. Lower QOL and high COL is one such explanation.

C. Higher Quality Work Force

Larger urban areas may have a larger proportion of industries which require a highly skilled or trained work force. Since higher skilled or higher quality labor receives higher wages, one would then find a relationship between city size and wages. This however would not be a "real" wage differential between areas but only a differential reward to labor of different quality.

Although this is a possible explanation, when one examines differences in wages paid workers in very narrowly defined occupations in different areas, one finds the same differentials by city size.** The Bureau of Labor statistics regularly reports on wages in different urban areas for certain carefully and technically defined occupations. The occupations are so defined in order to eliminate as much as possible the impact that skill, training and job content can have on wages paid. Statistical analysis of these data shows the same impact on urban size on wage differentials as reported above. This suggests that labor quality or occupational differences are not the explanation.

D. Oligopsony

In small towns and rural areas there may be only one or a few firms which supply most of the area's non-farm jobs while in moderate-to-large sized towns there would be many alternative employers. In such a situation, the firms in the small towns could take advantage of their dominant position and pay lower wages while firms in larger cities are limited by competition from doing so. This could produce a wage differential by city size. This differential, however, could only be temporary, for some workers would abandon the low-wage area and

---

*Robert S. Goldfarb and Anthony M.J. Yezer, "Evaluating Alternative Theories of Inter City and Interregional Wage Differentials," Journal of Regional Science 16, no. 3 (December 1976): 353.

**Victor Fuchs, Differentials in Hourly Earnings by Region and City Size, 1959. Occasional Paper 101, 1961, Columbia University Press. See also: Goldfarb and Yezer, op. cit.

outmigration would eliminate the differential. This cannot be
an explanation for a wage differential that has been stable
and persistent over time. Further, it suggests that the differential should exist only for quite small and rural areas.
Among larger cities (over say 100,000 population), where there
is a broader range of employment opportunities, the wage differential by size should disappear. It does not. Goldfarb
and Yezer, testing exactly this hypothesis, are led to reject
it as a substantial explanation of the observed differentials.*

E. Costs Associated with Migration

     In the discussion so far we have assumed that migration
is costless, that when a higher real level or total income is
available elsewhere, some part of the population migrates to
take advantage of it. This migration eliminates the differences between areas. If, however, there are costs associated
with migration other than the loss of a preferred location,
costs, for instance, associated with travel, moving, risk of
unemployment or even lower wages, learning about a new area,
etc., then real income must rise above a certain level before
migration will take place. The discounted value of the higher
income has to be sufficient to cover the costs associated with
migration. Differences below this level can develop without
any migration resulting. In this situation, wage differentials can develop and persist over time. The costs of migration create barriers to labor flows which allow "surpluses" of
labor to develop in some areas and "shortages" in others. The
size of the wage differentials would be tied to the size of
the migration barriers (costs).
     For these wage differentials to vary by city size in the
way observed, either of two additional assumptions is needed.
Either smaller cities must be the ones from which outmigration
is made necessary by changed economic conditions or migration
costs must be higher for migration from smaller cities or
both. Both assumptions are plausible. If large cities have
been displacing smaller cities as centers of economic activity
and/or if the relative isolation of small cities increases
moving costs and decreases the information available on alternative job opportunities, we would find persistent wage differentials between cities of different sizes.
     It should be noted that the migration costs being dis-
cussed here are not the costs associated with the loss of a
preferred local way-of-life, local amenities, local social
structure, regional culture, etc. These valued local features
which would be lost through migration are real costs but are
constituents of the "quality of life" and therefore to the extent they help create wage differentials are part of the

---

*Goldfarb and Yezer, op. cit.

"compensation payment" explanation. Here we are discussing migration costs unassociated with the loss of characteristics specific to a particular area. One also has to question the necessary assumption that smaller cities have faced more economic dislocation than larger cities and therefore that migration has been "required" from smaller to larger cities. Data cited above indicates that the opposite has been true: migration has been from the larger to the smaller cities.

Finally, the size of the wage differentials would seem to rule out this explanation. The migration costs are one-time costs experienced when migration takes place. Wage differentials represent income losses which are incurred every year that migration does not take place. Income differentials between cities of different sizes are substantial as indicated by Table 2.3. Wage differentials show similar but somewhat smaller differences.* If one takes "modest" differential of 20 percent and uses an annual wage of $8,000, each year the worker in the low-wage area did not migrate to the higher wage area, (s)he would lose $1,600. For a young worker (18 to 30 years) with a 40-year work life ahead, this annual loss would have a present value of $27,455 at a 5% discount rate, $15,640 at a 10% rate, and $6,400 at a 25% discount rate.** Thus migration costs to the young work force would have to be very substantial before they could explain significant wage differentials. Note that only the more mobile part of the popula-

Table 2.3

INCOME DIFFERENTIAL BETWEEN

CITIES OF DIFFERENT SIZES

SMSA Population x_{10}^3	Per Capita Personal Income Index 1972
0 to 250	100
250 to 500	109
500 to 1000	118
1000 to 2500	123
2500 to 9000	140
9000 +	156

Source: Hoch, "City Size Effects," op. cit.

*See below. The wage differentials are approximately 10% per order of magnitude in size differences. So between NYC and a town of less than 10,000, there would be a 40% differential.

**Also see Richard F. Wertheimer II, The Monetary Rewards of Migration within the U.S., The Urban Institute, Wash., 1970.

tion need be considered, for only some of the work force need migrate to move wages toward equilibrium values. We need focus only on the costs to the marginal migrant. I know of no empirical evidence which would support the assertion that personal migration costs to the most mobile part of the population are of this order of magnitude. The evidence is quite the contrary. Johnson* for instance found that migration costs from rural areas to large cities can be recouped in a year or less. After that, substantial net returns are generated. This implies a return on the investment in moving costs much higher than on other "human capital" investments. Yet this is not sufficient to lure enough of the most mobile sectors of the population to move and eliminate the wage differences. Something other than moving costs has to be holding them to the smaller cities and rural areas.

6. QOL AND MIGRATION

The above discussion suggests that the most convincing explanation for the variation of money wages between cities of different sizes is the compensating wage differential theory which sees these wage differentials as resulting from individuals' evaluation of the differing QOL in cities and migration which equalizes total real income among cities. This conclusion is arrived at somewhat indirectly. Some economists have tried to directly relate regional differences in the QOL and migration patterns. These studies support the hypothesis that people do take into account the QOL in making their locational decisions.

Cebula and Curran** found a statistically significant impact of climate (temperature) on migration rates for the seventy largest SMSAs between 1960 and 1970. Taxes and school expenditures were also important in explaining migration rates. Cebula and Vedder (as corrected by Graves) found that while climate was significantly related to migration for the thirty-nine largest SMSAs between 1960 and 1970, other amenity variables such as indices of particulate pollution and crime were

---

*Paul R. Johnson, "Labor Mobility: Some Costs and Returns," in Rural Poverty in the United States, a report by the President's National Advisory Commission on Rural Poverty (Washington: Government Printing Office) p. 247.

**R.J. Cebula and Christopher Curran, "Property Taxation and Human Migration," American Journal of Economics and Sociology 37, no. 1 (January 1978): 43-49.

not.* However, in both studies the more traditional economic variables such as unemployment rates and income levels were the most powerful explanators. We will see below that other studies raise doubts about the importance of these economic variables in migration decisions.

Ben-chieh Liu used indices of economic, social, and environmental condition in the fifty states in 1970 to try to explain net migration rates 1960-1970.** These various indices are discussed below. Each index combines data on many variables in a somewhat arbitrary way. He found that conventional economic variables such as relative family income and unemployment were not statistically significant explanators of migration rates while his QOL index was. The QOL index by itself, however, explained only 8 percent of the variation in migration rates. His index of "economic status" in an area was statistically significant. It combined with his other indices of "individual status" ("opportunity to develop oneself"), health and welfare, and educational development (all statistically significant) explained 45 percent of the variation in migration rates.

These indices, although not correlated with conventional economic variables such as income and unemployment, do lean heavily on traditional economic variables and do not seem, as a whole, to encompass what most mean by the "quality of life." However, Liu's work does show that variables which try to broadly encompass and describe the character of living in a particular area appear to be more powerful explanators of migration than the more narrowly defined economic variables.*** This supports the proposition that people do evaluate the QOL in making locational decisions.

---

*Richard J. Cebula and Richard K. Vedder, "A Note on Migration, Economic Opportunity, and the Quality of Life," Journal of Regional Science 13, no. 2 (1973): 107-111. Also see the comment correction and reply in Journal of Regional Science 16, no. 1 (April 1976): 109-115. The econometric methods used are of doubtful validity. Although a simultaneous equation model is developed each equation is estimated individually ignoring the simultaneity bias. The effect of this on the estimates is left unanalyzed.

**"Differential Net Migration Rates and the Quality of Life," Review of Economics and Statistics LVII, no. 3 (August 1975): 324-337.

***An alternative explanation of the poor performance of traditional economic variables in explaining net migration will be discussed below. Outmigration may not be much affected by economic variables while inmigration is. The effect on *net* migration may thus be obscured.

3
The Theory of Compensating Wage Differentials: A Formal Analysis

1. INTRODUCTION

In this Chapter we more formally develop the arguments of the last Chapter that the observed wage differentials between areas can be used as an objective measure of how people in the aggregate value the relative QOL in those areas.

The discussion will be in terms of technical economic and econometric theory. The non-economist may wish to move quickly through this Chapter getting a feel only for the assumptions which have to be made to reach the conclusions discussed in the previous Chapter. This Chapter can be skipped in its entirety without interrupting the basic line of argument.

2. THE FORMAL MODEL

We assume a competitive economy consisting of a system of cities in which firms locate on the basis of the favorable attributes a particular city has for the firms' productive activities and labor is perfectly mobile. Each city is assumed to be small relative to total system of cities so that change in one city has only marginal impacts on the whole system. We assume that each city has an identically shaped short-run labor supply curve reflecting similar mixes of peoples with disutility for work and/or utility for leisure or non-market activity. In this situation the relative position of each city's short-run labor supply curve will depend upon the importance of variables other than money wages in individuals' total incomes and the size of the work force (population). The differences in the former causes differences in the vertical position; differences in the latter affect the horizontal position. Thus in Figure 3.1 we show the short-run labor supply curves for two equal-sized cities, A and B. If labor supply is a function of money wage and the value of the local quality of life (VQ), where QOL includes the local cost of

living, we can write:
$$S = S (W, VQ).$$

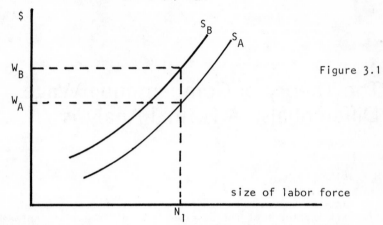

Figure 3.1

In Figure 3.1, city B has a lower QOL or higher COL $(VQ_A \quad VQ_B)$, and it thus takes a higher wage W_B to provide individuals with the same total real income which elicits a labor supply of N_1 workers. The wage difference provides identical total real incomes to individuals in both cities.
$$W_B + VQ_B = W_A + VQ_B = TI \text{ or } W_B - W_A = VQ_A - VQ_B.$$

If both cities have identical demand curves,* this difference in QOL would lead to a wage differential between the cities. Figure 3.2 shows this. The wage differential, $W_B - W_A$, will be less than the difference in the value of the

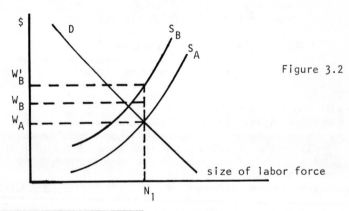

Figure 3.2

---

*This assumption only simplifies the graphs. It is not necessary for any of the primary conclusions.

QOL, $VQ_A - VQ_B = W'_B - W_A$. This has led one observer to argue that wage differentials will understate the difference in the value of the QOL if the demand for labor has any elasticity at all.* Although this is true in the short-run when migration is not allowed, we will see that it is not true once long-run adjustments are allowed.

If labor is perfectly mobile, in the long run each city faces perfectly elastic horizontal labor supply at a level of total real income (or welfare) that is common to all areas. If one area were, through its particular combination of QOL, COL and money wages, to provide a lower level of total real income than available elsewhere, it would lose all of its work force. If it were to provide a higher level of total real incomes, all workers would migrate to that city. Thus for city A and city B long-run equilibrium requires

$$TI_A = W_A + VQ_A = TI_B = W_B + VQ_B = \overline{TI}$$

If the value of the QOL varies with city size, say for the sake of argument with large cities having a higher valued QOL, VA might vary with city size as shown at the bottom of Figure 3.3. This will cause the observed money wage long run labor supply curve to deviate from the perfectly elastic total income long run supply curve $\overline{TI}$ as shown in Figure 3.2. The difference between $\overline{TI}$ and LRS being the money wage compensation necessary to keep total income the same. LRS = $\overline{TI}$ - VA.

If in this situation wage levels, as determined by short-run supply and demand conditions, were lower in small cities than in large cities ($W_{S_1} < W_{L_1}$, in Figure 3.3), this would be a disequalibrium, unstable situation with the level of well being lower in the small city than in the large city.

$$W_{S_1} + VA_{S_1} < \overline{TI} < W_{L_1} + VA_{L_1}$$

Migration would take place from the area of lower total income, the smaller city, to the area of higher well being, the larger city. This migration is indicated in Figure 3.3 by the shifting short-run supply curves. Migration would stop and equilibrium established only when each city had moved to a point on LRS. Here total incomes would be identical and the wage difference, now revised, $W_{S_2} - W_{L_2}$, would be an accurate measure of the difference in the value of the QOL, $VA_{L_2} - VA_{S_2}$.

---

*Lester C. Thurow, "Psychic Income: Useful or Useless," American Economic Review 68 (May 1978): 142-148.

Figure 3.3

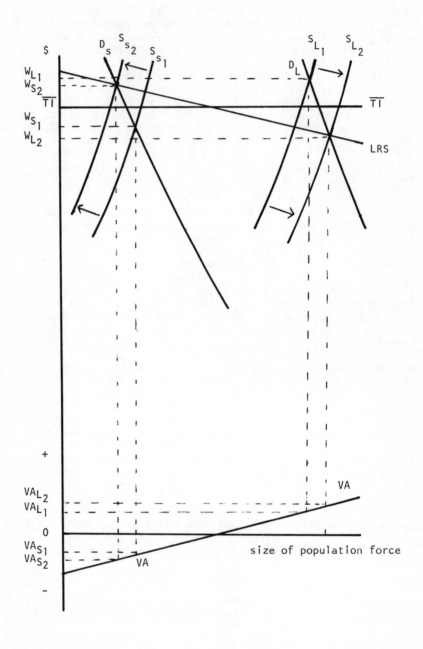

3. ALLOWING FOR INDIVIDUAL VARIATIONS IN THE EVALUATION OF ENVIRONMENTAL RESOURCES

In the previous section we have implicitly assumed that all individuals make the same judgment about the relative value of the services the environment in a particular area provides. This is too restrictive for it obscures some important impacts of changes in the flow of services from the environment. It seems to suggest that whatever happens to the environment, changes in money wages will fully compensate individuals so as to keep them at the same level of well-being. This is not the case. This section will refine the argument in order to demonstrate this.

One would expect individuals' tastes for a particular area's environment to be distributed over some range. Figure 3.4 suggests a way in which individuals' judgments about the value of the differences in a particular area's environment (ΔVQ) might be distributed. The distribution indicates that on average the area has a more highly valued quality of life although a minority do not think so.

If this frequency distribution is given by
$$n = f(\Delta VQ)$$
where n is the number of individuals who evaluate the areas environmental services as having a value ΔVQ higher than elsewhere.

If we assume that individuals locate in this area in order of the strength of their preferences, this function can be transformed into the equivalent of a demand function for this area's environmental services by starting with those individuals who most highly value the area's environment (those with differential values ΔVQ max) and accumulating those individuals with successively lower evaluations of the advantages of

Figure 3.4

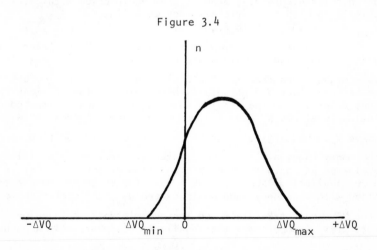

the advantages of living in the area. This involves a cumulative summation of individuals

$$N = \int_{i=\Delta VQ_{max}}^{i=\Delta VQ} i \, di$$

where N is the total number of individuals who evaluate the differential value of this particular environment as worth at least as much as ΔVQ. This gives us a new function which when plotted with ΔVQ as a function of population has a shape similar to that shown in Figure 3.5.

Figure 3.5

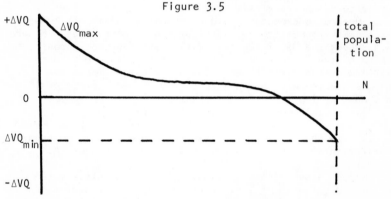

If we assume that the area we are focusing on is small relative to the nation so that migration to or from that area has no measurable impact on the labor supply, equilibrium wages, and environmental quality elsewhere, we can incorporate this distribution of tastes for the area's environment into our earlier diagrams by drawing the ΔVQ function with $\Delta VQ = 0$ coinciding with the national money wage line $W_{nat} = \overline{TI} - VQ_{nat}$ as in Figure 3.6.

As long as the money wage paid in Area "A" is higher than $0 \, VQ_{max}$, some individuals would be receiving a total real income higher than that available elsewhere in the nation because they place a particularly high value on the services they receive from the Area "A" environment. Thus, if the population level was N_o and the money wage level in Area "A" were above W_o, the marginal migrant would receive in addition to the money wage, a flow of environmental services which (s)he evaluates as worth rs more than the flow of environmental services available elsewhere, $\Delta VQ = rs$. The value of these combined with the money wage would exceed W_{nat} and migration to Area "A" would take place and the new migrants would enjoy a total real income above that available elsewhere. At a popu-

Figure 3.6

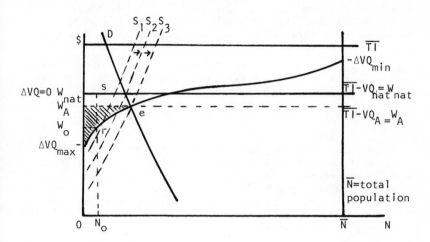

lation level as low as N_o, and a wage as low as W_o, labor demand will exceed supply and money wages will rise well above
W_o, thus encouraging additional migration. The labor supply
curve will shift to the right.

Inmigration will continue as long as the combination of
money wage and differential value of environmental services
(ΔVQ) exceeds the money wage available nationally, W_{nat}. As
migration continues, the differential value of Area "A'''s QOL
to the marginal migrant falls. The inmigration will stop when
the money wage in Area "A", W_A, plus the differential value of
environmental services, ΔVQ, equal the national wage, W_{nat},
that is where supply and demand intersect at the point where
ΔVQ cuts the demand curve. At that point "e",

$$W_A + \Delta VQ = W_{nat} \text{ and}$$

$$W_A + \Delta VQ + VQ_{nat} = W_{nat} + VQ_{nat} = \overline{TI}$$

Thus the incentive for inmigration vanishes. The difference
in money wages $W_{nat} - W_A = \Delta VQ$: at the margin wage differentials exactly compensate for QOL differentials between areas.
This is the result we obtained above, but now the result applies only to the marginal migrant. Note that at equilibrium,
all Area "A" residents except the last to migrate are receiving total real incomes above the national average. This "surplus" is the shaded area in Figure 3.6.

Figure 3.7 shows this equilibrium in more detail. If as a result of environmental change, Area "A's" environment became indistinguishable from the national norm, the ΔVQ curve would become a straight line coinciding with $\Delta VQ = 0$ and the W_{nat} line. In such a situation Area "A" would appear to be the same as any other "average" part of the nation and individuals would have no preferences with respect to it. The frequency function would degenerate into a vertical line at $\Delta VQ = 0$ and ΔVQ function would become a horizontal line at $\Delta VQ = 0$. In Figures 3.6 and 3.7, the ΔVQ function would degenerate into the W_{nat} line.

In this situation, outmigration would take place from Area "A" because the money wages are below national averages and the environment does not compensate for this lower money income. The outmigration would cause the supply curve to shift to the left. With a smaller labor supply money wages in Area "A" would increase until they were equal to what was available elsewhere in the economy, W_{nat}.

As a result of the environmental change $N_1 - N_2$ workers leave Area "A" and go elsewhere but earn wherever they go at least the total real wage equal to $\overline{TI}$ earned at the margin in Area "A" before the change and, if they go to an average area, earn money wages equal to W_{nat}. Thus $N_2 N_1 be_2$ continues to be earned elsewhere by the outmigrants. However, these outmigrants while in Area "A" enjoyed an additional income of dce_1. That is, all but the very marginal worker in Area "A" enjoyed a total real income above $\overline{TI}$. For those forced to leave and move to an average area cde_1 is lost. The higher money wages, W_{nat}, in the new location do not compensate for that loss. For

Figure 3.7

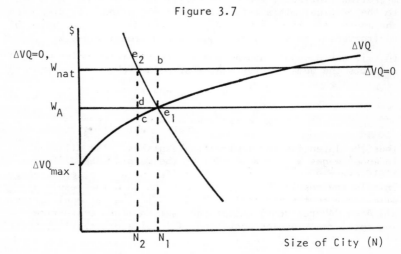

those who do not move, wages increase from W_A to W_{nat}. But
this just compensates for the environmental losses of equal
amount. At the same time an amount of value equal to ΔVQ_{max}
cdw_A, the remaining original intra-marginal value of living in
Area "A", is lost and not compensated for by higher money
wages.

Thus an amount $\Delta VQ_{max} W_A e_1$ is on net lost as a result of
the environmental change.

Note that although at the margin residents of Area "A"
are no better off or no worse off than the nation, both earn
a total real income of $\overline{TI}$, Area "A" residents *are* worse off.
They have suffered a net loss for which no compensation is
provided. The reason for the net loss is that those who like
Area "A" move to Area "A". Those who do not like its unique
aspects never move there. Thus the changes in environment in
the direction of the national norm benefit no one (those who
prefer that are not here) but hurt those who are here. The
adjustments at the margin do not eliminate this net loss.

4. THE USE OF COMPENSATING WAGE DIFFERENCES

Economists studying the value of the QOL have used two
quite different methods. One has estimated the value of
changes in the environment of an area by studying changes in
property values within cities. If the environment in part of
the city has been improved, say by reducing air pollution or
crime, individuals should be willing, to the extent that they
value these improvements, to pay more for the now more attractive properties there. Thus by studying intracity variations
in amenities and property values, economists have tried to
estimate the value individuals place on those amenities.

The other method is the one we have discussed above: the
analysis of wage differentials between areas and the interpretation of these as compensation for differences in the
value of amentities in those areas.

Each method by itself is incomplete for each assumes the
adjustment process is either only through property values or
only through wage adjustments while the other remains un-
changed. In general, when there is a change in the QOL in an
area, wages and property values and the overall level of welfare can be expected to change. The full value of the change
is not summarized by any one of these except under very restrictive conditions. If, for instance, a city substantially
improves its physical environment, the first impact may be on
land rents in the areas most substantially improved. With
enough time to allow migration, people will move to this now
relatively superior city causing wages to fall in that city
and rise, relatively, in the cities they are moving away from.
Due to the influx of individuals, rents will rise throughout

34

the improved city and fall in the cities losing population.
Thus the effects of the improvement will be decreased wages
and increased costs of living (increased rents) in the improved city and higher levels of welfare in other cities due
to rising wages and falling rents. The value of the improvement cannot be measured by the change in wages in the improved
city for some of it has been swallowed up by rent increases
and some of it has been exported to other areas via rising
wages in those other areas.

This interdependence between economic variables and economic regions has three important implications:

A. Although we may be able to use wage differentials
to estimate   the *differences between* regions in the value of
the QOL, we cannot estimate the value of a *change in* the value
of the QOL.

B. QOL changes and COL changes (housing costs being an
important part) must both be studied and may not be separable.

C. Migration does not result in an optimal distribution of population and level of local amenities. Wage differentials do not fully compensate individuals for a degraded
QOL.

The last point was discussed in section 3 of Chapter 2
aobve. Here we will discuss the first two points in turn.

A. The Value of Changes in the QOL vs
The Value of Differences in the QOL

In general, in a world where the level of welfare depends
upon money wages, the level of non-marketed amenities, the mix
of goods consumed (including housing services and transportation) and the prices of goods (including the price of housing
and transportation), an improvement in the QOL will, in the
new general equilibrium established after all adjustments have
been made, result in changes in land rents, expenditures on
transportation and housing, the mix of goods consumed, wages,
and the overall level of well-being. No one change will sum-
marize the value of the change in QOL. Polinsky and Rubinfeld[*] show, through intuitive examples, that it is possible
that the "expected case" of wages falling and housing costs
rising as a result of an improvement in the QOL may not take
place. No general results can be stated. In addition, Courant and Rubinfeld[**] show that the migration of factors of production which a change in the QOL triggers causes changes in

[*]A. Mitchell Polinsky and Daniel L. Rubinfeld, "The Long-Run
Effects of a Residential Property Tax and Local Public Services," Journal of Urban Economics 5 (1978): 241-262.

[**]Paul N. Courant and Daniel L. Rubinfeld, "On the Measurement
of Benefits in an Urban Context: Some General Equilibrium Issues," Journal of Urban Economics (forthcoming, July 1978).

supply conditions elsewhere in the economy. Thus the change has welfare impacts beyond the original area. These total impacts will not, on net, be zero and will not be captured by a study of the changes in economic variables in the original area.

Our analysis aims at establishing a value for the QOL in a particular area and discussing how policy decisions which affect the QOL can take into account this impact. What the discussion above points out is that all that the analysis of compensating wage differentials can tell us is the *difference* in the value of the QOL (including COL) in a particular area. This is important information in judging the value of what a particular area's residents have to protect, but it is also restrictive. It does not allow us to study those wage differentials to establish what the value of a *change* in the QOL would be, and that is what is important from a policy perspective. However, if the area being studied is small relative to the national economy and our interest is in the value of a change in the QOL to that area's residents, not the total value to all residents in the nation, the situation is not all that frustrating. Changes in an area which is small relative to the national economy, almost no matter what their size, will have little impact outside of that area. Further, we are not interested, in this analysis, in the benefits or costs an area imposes on the rest of the nation. Thus we can attempt to project the value of degradation or improvements in an area's QOL (including COL) using the analysis of compensating wage differences.

B. QOL and COL Changes

We have discussed earlier the reasons for believing that both QOL decreases and COL increases with urban size and density. The discussion above indicates that improvements in the quality of life may be accompanied by increased property values and thus the cost of housing and business location or the cost of transportation. Compensating wage differences in maintaining a common total real income in all areas will adjust to cover both QOL and COL differences. Without detailed COL indices for each city which take into account the higher housing costs and/or the larger distances traveled, etc. (which are *not* available), there is no way we can separate out what part of the wage differential is compensation for QOL and what part for COL. Since we are primarily interested in *differences* in the level of welfare between areas, this is not totally frustrating to our purposes. But it does place limits on how far we can proceed with the interpretation of wage differences.

5. ECONOMETRIC ESTIMATION OF COMPENSATING WAGE DIFFERENTIALS

In the following, we specify the simultaneous equation model implicit in much of the literature on compensating wage differentials and then indicate why estimation of a single reduced form equation by ordinary least squares is an appropriate technique.

Let the labor supply be a function of money, wages and the value of the quality of life in an urban area. Let size of population (P), population density (D), and the percent of the population in urban areas (U) be proxies for the QOL in an urban area. Then the labor supply equation is:

$$L^S = L \ (W, D, U, P)$$

If firms' production functions are CES functions and we allow agglomeration economies of larger cities to boost labor productivity, the value added by an individual firm, S_i, is given by:

$$S_i = [b \ (\alpha L_i)^{-B} + (1-b)K_i^{-B}]^{-1/B}$$

where L is labor, K is capital, and α is the effect of agglomeration economics on labor. If we write the first order conditions for profit maximizing use of labor (value of the marginal product of labor equal to wage) we can derive a labor demand curve.*

$$L_i = S_i \ (b\alpha^{-B})^{\frac{1}{(B+1)}} \ W^{-\frac{1}{(B+1)}}$$

If the agglomerative effect is tied primarily to the size of the total work force in the area, we can let $\alpha = L^\gamma$ and sum the firms' labor demand functions over all firms to get the labor demand for the city

$$L^d = S^{\frac{B+1}{\gamma B+B+1}} \ b^{(\gamma B+B+1)} \ W^{\frac{1}{-\gamma B+B+1}}$$

or in log form

$$\log L^d = C_d + a_1 \log W + a_2 \log S$$

where C_d is a constant.

This, if we put the labor supply function in log linear form, gives us the following equation system

$$\log L^D = C_d + a_1 \log W + a_2 \log S$$

$$\log L^S = C_s + b_1 \log W + b_2 \log D + b_3 \log U + b_4 \log P$$

Kelley** has argued that to estimate the effect of urban

---

*See Kevin C. Kelley, "Urban Disamenities and the MEW," Journal of Urban Economics 4 (1977): 381-82.

**Kelley, op. cit.

QOL on wages, one must recognize the simultaneous effect of both labor supply factors (urban QOL) on wages and labor demand influences. Wages are simultaneously determined by both supply and demand. To ignore the demand side will produce biased results.

Kelley* urges the use of two stage-least squares, the first stage of which involves regressing the "endogenous" variable (wages) on all of the "exogenous" variables

$$\log W = C_W + d_1 \log S + d_2 \log D + d_3 \log U + d_4 \log P$$

This regression yields a "predicted value" for log W, $\widehat{\log W}$, which in the second stage is substituted into the supply and demand equations

$$\log L^d = C_d + a_1 \ (\widehat{\log W}) + a_2 \log S$$

$$\log L^S = C_s + b_1 \ (\widehat{\log W}) + b_2 \log D + b_3 \log U + b_4 \log P$$

These then can be estimated singly using ordinary least squares.

Most other econometric analyses of the impact of urban disamenities on wages have simply regressed wages on measures of disamenities or amenities thus ignoring the role of labor demand. In the above equations this amounts to dropping the log of value added from the first stage estimating equation and then accepting the coefficients on the disamenity variables as accurate measures of the coefficients in the labor supply equation. Both of these steps are incorrect and introduce bias to the estimates of the value of the disamenities. Kelley proceeds with two stage-least squares estimation and gets results which contradict most of the previous work: large urban areas provide amenities not disamenities; the QOL is higher in large, densely populated urban areas.

There are several serious flaws in Kelley's approach: (A) He treats output levels as exogenous when it is not; (B) He ignores the long-run equilibrium conditions of the model; (C) He ignores the high colinearity between total value added in manufacturing in an urban area and size of population. Each of these will discussed in turn.

A. The level of output of firms is no more exogenous than their level of employment of labor or the wages paid. Firms choose the level of output and the level of employment of inputs simultaneously. Thus the equation system above is incomplete. It does not indicate what determines the level of output S. This is forced on the model by the choice of a linear homogenous production function (constant returns to scale). With such a production function marginal costs are constant and the level of output is indeterminant. Thus one

---

*Kelley, op. cit., p. 383.

has to take output as given even though this makes no theoretical sense.

The minimum simultaneous equation system which economic theory would allow in this situation is the following:

(1) $L^D = L^D$ (W, S, P)

(2) $L^S = L^S$ (W, P, D, U)

(3) $\overline{P}_{output_i} = MC_{output_i} = f$ (S_i, MP_{L_i}, MP_{k_i}, W, r)

(4) $L^S = L^D$

Equations (1) and (2) are simply supply and demand equations with population size included in the demand equation to account for agglomeration economies. Equation (3) determines output for each firm by having each firm increase output until marginal cost (which is determined by level of output, the productivity of inputs, and input costs) equals the exogenously determined output price. In the above system, population, density, urbanization, wages, interest rate, and output prices are exogenous. The marginal products of labor and capital are the first partial derivatives of the production function and thus are functions of the level of factor input use. The endogenous variables are wage and level of output.

With this set of equations, two stage-least squares requires first the regression of the endogenous variables on all of the exogenous variables

$W = f$ (P, D, U, P_{output})

$S = g$ (P, D, U, P_{output})

The inclusion of P_{output} points out a serious aggregation problem with equations (3). Output levels are determined by each firm as they equate product price and marginal costs. There is no city-wide "product price." Thus equations (3) cannot be aggregated to establish a city-wide relationship. Dropping P_{output} from the above first stage estimation will bias the results only if P_{output} is correlated with the city size, density, and urbanization variables. This seems unlikely. Thus a first stage stimation of

$\log W = C_W + d_1 \log D + d_2 \log U + d_3 \log P$ (5)

the type of equation estimated by most economists studying urban disamenity effects may well be appropriate. The level of output does not belong in the estimating equation.

B. We have available to us for our econometric estimation more information than is included in the above equation systems. Kelley's system is appropriate only in the short-run where equilibrium simply requires local labor supply to equal local

labor demand. But in a national economy with reasonably mobile labor, we have another long-run equilibrium condition:
the total real income of labor in all cities must be the same
or migration will take place. This amounts to specifying a
horizontal total income long-run labor supply equation such as
was discussed in Section 2 above. In such a model we know
that labor demand has no influence on wage differences. These
are determined entirely by differences in the value of QOL and
COL. Thus one could estimate the effect of various urban disamenities on these wage differences by ordinary least square.
No simultaneous equation system is needed.

Further, if one does regress wage levels (not differences)
on measures of urban disamenities as in equation (5) above,
there is no need to proceed with the second stage of the estimation process. The first stage estimates the impact of QOL
variables on wages. But in the short run this underestimates
the value of the QOL.

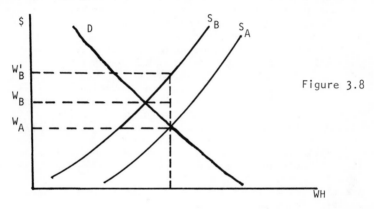

Figure 3.8

In Figure 3.8, we simplify the diagram by assuming a common labor demand curve. What we wish to estimate is the impact of QOL variables on labor supply, i.e., the vertical distance between the two supply curves $(W_B' - W_A)$. The interaction of supply and demand establish a wage difference of only
$W_B - W_A$. Thus simply relating disamenities to wages will not
accurately indicate the value of the QOL. To get at this we
need to proceed with the second stage estimation which actually estimates the shift parameters on the labor supply curve
associated with the different measures of urban disamenities.
However, in long-run equilibrium, as shown in Section 2 above,
the observed wage difference *will* equal $W_B' - W_A$. When migration is allowed for, the bias we are worried about here, that
caused by the elasticity of labor demand, is eliminated. The
situation is that shown in Figure 3.3 above.

C. As pointed out above, from an econometric point of view,
the level of output does not belong in the first stage estimation of the wage equation: it is not an exogenous variable.
Its presence also causes seriously multicolinearity problems,
for the simple correlation coefficient between the size of
city and value-added-in manufacturing in that city is 0.94 for
the data Kelley used! Thus the value-added-in manufacturing
variable is acting as a city size variable and should either
be treated as another measure of the disamenities associated
with cities (heavy industry and the pollution, noise, congestion, etc. which goes with it), in which case neither the coefficient on it or on size may be dependable, or it should be
dropped and the size variables allowed to reflect the full effects of urban size. A third possibility is that it is a better measure of urban-size disamenities and should be used in
place of population size. If the value-added-in manufacturing
is dropped from the wage equation, the population coefficient
indicates the same disamenity effects associated with size
which other studies have shown. The amenities Kelley found
associated with urban living disappear. This is indicated in
Table 3.1 where Kelley's equation is estimated with and without the level of output (value added) as an exogenous variable.
The urban size effect is indicated by the coefficient on the
population variable, log P. In both equations, it is significant at the 99 percent level but has a negative sign indicating an amenity effect when the output variable, Q, is included in the equation but a positive sign indicating a disamenity when that variable is excluded.

Table 3.1 also shows the effect of dropping the population variable and retaining the value-added variable as an alternative measure of size. This provides an alternative interpretation of Kelley's results: the coefficient on value-added
measures the urban disamenity. It is strongly significant and
the equation has a much higher R^2 than that using population
as the size variable. Given that the sample is of wages and
value added in manufacturing, it would not be surprising to
find that the level of *manufacturing* output was a good size
measure for studies of urban disamenities, for many of the
environmental problems most discussed are associated with
heavy industry and many of the social problems which most dis-
tress people are associated with the older decaying manufacturing centers.

When different preferences are allowed for, as pointed
out above, we still obtain the earlier result that wage differentials accurately reflect the difference in the value of
an area's QOL, but now the result only applies to the evaluation of the marginal migrant. (See page 31). If this evaluation by the marginal migrant differs substantially from those
held by the rest of the population, this wage differential
will not be a good estimate of the value of this area's QOL as
seen by others. Figure 3.9 presents one extreme where the ΔVQ

Table 3.1

Regression Results With and Without Value Added as an Exogenous Variable[a]

$$\log W = 0.3312 + 0.1495 \log Q - 0.0636 \log D + 0.2231 \log U - .0941 \log \text{Popul} \qquad R^2$$
$$(9.977) \qquad (-4.690) \qquad (2.886) \qquad (-5.170) \qquad 0.35152$$

$$\log W = 0.2976 \qquad\qquad + 0.01252 \log D - .0666 \log U + .04667 \log \text{Popul} \qquad 0.07719$$
$$(.9385) \qquad (-.7816) \qquad (3.409)$$

$$\log W = 0.2428 + 0.0894 \log Q - 0.0486 \log D + 0.0583 \log U \qquad 0.2778$$
$$(8.97) \qquad (-3.48) \qquad (.79)$$

[a]Observations: 240 SMSA's from the City-County Data Book, 1970, U.S. Bureau of the Census, Table 3. Student t values shown in the parentheses.

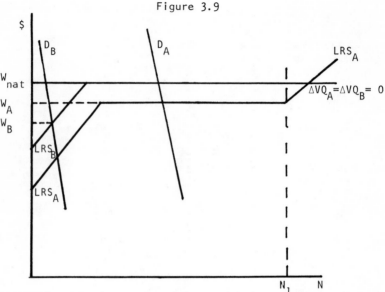

Figure 3.9

curves for two cities, A and B, are labeled as long-run supply
curves LRS_B and LRS_A. Here, if the vertical distance between
LRS_B and LRS_A, is a constant for populations less than N_1 we
could argue that city A, at least until the population surpass-
ed N_1 has a higher quality of life in the sense that for populations less than N_1 individuals would pay more to enjoy it
than to enjoy city B's QOL. But if because city B had very few
advantages for production, the labor demand might by very low
(D_B) while city A, if it had significantly more production advantages might face a much higher labor demand, D_A. The result would be a wage differential, $W_A > W_B$, which might be mis-
interpreted to mean city B has the higher quality of life when
the opposite was true. Simultaneous equation econometric techniques which estimated the actual distance between the LRS
curves rather than the equilibrium wage differentials would be
called for. This result follows from the existence in the situation pictured in Figure 3.9 of a small minority who prefer
city B while the vast majority see that city B is no different
than the national average and labor demand being so low in
that city to offer employment only to that minority.

If instead, the distribution of preferences were more uniform and generated LRS curves such as those in Figure 3.10,
this situation could not exist. Wage differentials would be
unaffected by labor demand and the previous results would hold:
single equation estimates would not be biased. Which situa-

tion actually exists in the real world is, of course, an empirical question which will not be investigated here.

Figure 3.10

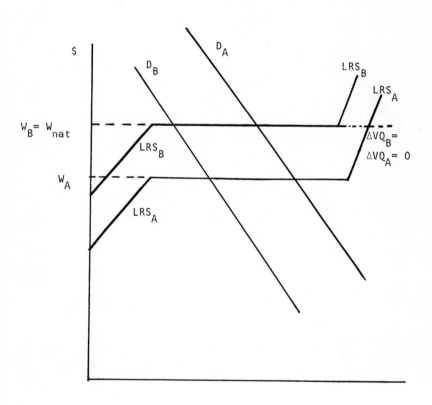

4
The Size of Compensating Wage Differentials and an Application

1. HOW WAGES VARY BY SIZE OF CITY

In this Chapter the results of statistical analysis of wage differentials between urban areas are reported. Despite the use of different definitions of "wages" and the use of different samples of the population, a common conclusion results: each order of magnitude (factor of ten) increase in population size is associated with an increase in wages by approximately 10 percent.

The appropriate definition of "wages" for this sort of analysis is not obvious. Most labor market analysis seeks a dollar wage per-hour-worked measure, possibly adjusted for the value of fringe benefits. This is the money income measure most obviously associated with a job and the one upon which job seekers are assumed to focus. However, in making locational decisions, families may be interested in a broader indicator of opportunities for a second (or third) family job, overtime work, part-time jobs, etc. Data on median family income or per capita personal income may provide a better measure of these broader income opportunities than hourly wage levels in a particular oppupation. On the other hand, both of these alternative measures include non-labor income (property income) which is not likely to be related to QOL or migration. In addition, per capita measures allow regional differences in family size to affect the measure in a way that is irrelevant to a family's locational decision. Thus none of the measures are exactly appropriate and we report on results using each of them. Table 4.1 summarizes the variety of statistical analyses that have been carried out.

The results presented in Table 4.1 are given in terms of the impact on wages of "order of magnitude" changes in population. "Order of magnitude" is used in this paper not in the colloquial sense of "about the same size" but in the scientific sense of "ten fold." Thus 10,000 is an "order of magnitude" larger than 1,000 but an "order of magnitude" smaller

45

Table 4.1

THE SIZE OF COMPENSATING WAGE DIFFERENTIALS

Study	Effect of Population Sizes on Wages	Definition of Wages	Method and Variables Used	Data Source and Year
Hoch 1	4% per order of magnitude	hourly wage as reported by worker	no regression analysis. Simple averaging of wages for cities in different size categories. The sample is of migrants and their wages after a move.	Social Security Administration (1965)
Hoch 2	7-13% per order of magnitude; 9.4% is the average	hourly wage as reported by firm for narrowly defined occupations	the wage for each occupation is regressed on the log of population and a regional dummy representing the South	BLS Area Wage Surveys 25 SMSA's (1966-70)
Hoch 3	6.5% per order of magnitude	same	additional variables are added to the regression: % black, city density, and climate	same (1966-70)
Hoch 4	16% per order of magnitude	per capita personal income	per capita income regressed on population size and dummies for the major census regions	231 SMSA's Bureau of Eco. Analysis (1972)

Table 4.1 - continued

Study	Effect of Population Sizes on Wages	Definition of Wages	Method and Variables Used	Data Source and Year
Hoch 5	1929:26% per order of magnitude 1940:22% per order of magnitude 1950:13% per order of magnitude	same	same	same (1929-50)
Goldfarb 1	1% per additional 10,000 employed (average)	hourly wage as reported by firm for narrowly defined occupations	regression of wage on size of total employment in the SMSA and a non-South dummy	BLS Area Wage surveys 44-66 SMSA's (1973)
Goldfarb 2	1.6% per 10,000 employed above 40,000 employed size	same	the equation was allowed to become non-linear at 40,000 total employment	same
Goldfarb 3	1.4% per 10,000 for size between 0-40,000 and 1.3% per 10,000 for size between 40,000-100,000 very small effect for size beyond this	same	the equation was allowed to become non-linear at 40,000; 100,000; 300,000; and 1,000,000 in total employment	same

Table 4.1 - continued

Study	Effect of Popula- tion Sizes on Wages	Definition of Wages	Method and Variables Used	Data Source and Year
Gold- farb 4	9% per order of magnitude	same	putting his results in log linear terms	same
Meyer 1	12% per order of magnitude 17% if 4 largest SMSA's dropped	median family income divided by COL index	log of real median family income on migration, rate, log population size, log percent urban, log population density, log % block, log educational expenditures, log property tax, log educational index	BLS 39 SMSA's (1970)
Meyer 2	population coeffi- cient is not signi- ficant; only popula- tion density is	same	a "preferred" list of variables including the presence of univ- ersity or capital city, tempera- ture, association with water	same
Meyer 3	population coeffi- cient is not signi- ficant. Density is but is negative	wage rate for general occupa- tional categor- ies. Calculated by dividing wage bill by manhours.	same as Meyer 1	39 SMSA (1970)
Meyer 4	neither popula- tion nor density variables are significant	same	same as Meyer 2	same

Table 4.1 - continued

Study	Effect of Population Sizes and Wages	Definition of Wages	Method and Variables Used	Data Source and Year
Nordhaus	population coefficients not significant	median personal income	same as Meyer 1 but used county data for selected states	County Data City-County Data Book (1970)
Power 1	11.4% per order of magnitude	wage rate for manufacturing production workers, calculated by dividing wage bill by manhours	regression of log wage on log of population, log population density, log % urban	240 SMSA's City-County Data Book (1970)
Power 2	10.7% per order of magnitude	same	same with South-nonsouth dummy included	same
Kelley	Minus 20% per order of magnitude (larger cities associated with lower wages)	same	same as Power 1 with log of total value added in manufacturing included	221 SMSA's City-County Data Book (1970)

Source: Hoch 1-5: Irving Hoch, "Income and City Size," Urban Studies 9 (October 1972):244-328 and "Variations in the Quality of Urban Life Among Cities and Regions" in Wingo and Evans, Public Economics and the Quality of Life

Goldfarb 1-3: Robert S. Goldfarb and Anthony M.J. Yezer, "Evaluating Alternative Theories of Intercity and Interregional Wage Differentials," Journal of Regional Science 16

Meyer 1-4: John R. Meyer and Robert A. Leone, "The Urban Disamenity Revisited" in Wingo and Evans, Public Economics and the Quality of Life

50

Table 4.1 - continued

Source: Nordhaus: W. Nordhaus and J. Tobin, "Economic Growth," NBER 50th Anniversary Colloquium, Vol. V, Columbia University Press, New York, 1972.

Kelley: Kevin C. Kelley, "Urban Disamenities and the Measure of Economic Welfare," Journal of Urban Economics 4 (1977):379-388.

Power 1-2: Thomas M. Power, unpublished work, University of Montana, Missoula, Montana 59812.

than 100,000. The logarithm of a number gives a measure of its order of magnitude. The log of 1,000 is 3; the log of 10,000 is 4; the 100,000 is 5, etc. Each is one order of magnitude larger than the previous.

The use of money wage rate data (Hoch 2, Goldfarb 4, Power 1 and 2) results in wage differentials of about 10 percent per order to magnitude difference in city size. Use of median family income or per capita income (Hoch 4, Meyer 1) results in much larger differentials, approximately 16 percent per order of magnitude. If long lists of additional explanatory variables are added to the regressions (Nordhaus, Meyer 2, 3, 4), few if any of the variables have coefficients which are significantly different from zero. In particular, population size ceases to be a statistically significant explanator of the wage differences. Since many of the QOL variables are highly correlated with each other and with city size, this is not surprising. The statistical analysis cannot separate the variables from one another. Two studies report results indicating that urban size is associated, on net, with amenities not disamenities. Meyer's results are based upon the summing up of several coefficients, some of which are statistically not different from zero. The correct conclusion should have been that no measurable amenity effect was discovered. Kelley's results are based upon theoretical and econometric errors which are discussed in the previous Chapter.

The interpretation of the North-South regional differences is somewhat difficult. Because of the lower incomes associated with the south, inclusion of the south-nonsouth dummy variable results in a moderate reduction of the importance of population size in explaining wage differentials. Hoch thinks this is appropriate because the south still may have an excess supply of labor and the wage variations there may reflect that disequilibrium rather than differences in the QOL.* On the other hand, much of the manufacturing in the south is located outside of large urban areas, in smaller towns and rural areas.** Thus one of the primary reasons for the lower wages in the south is the size of the urban areas. Polzin*** found that the most powerful explanator of differences in manufacturing wage indices which had been standardized to account for

---

*Irving Hoch, "Variations in the Quality of Urban Life Among Cities and Regions," op. cit.

**Barry M. Moriaty, "A Note on the Unexplained Residuals in North-South Wage Differential Models," Journal of Regional Science 18, no. 1 (1978):105-108.

***Paul E. Polzin, "State and Regional Wage Differences," op. cit.

industry mix was the percentage of manufacturing located outside of the largest cities (standard metropolitan statistical
areas). This was true for both the North and the South. These
results confirm Fuchs' earlier conclusions that after all adjustments are made for labor quality, region, industry mix,
etc., differences in wages vary strongly with size of place.
Moriaty, Polzin, and Fuchs all attribute this to excess labor
supply in small towns. However, as argued above, this explanation is not very convincing. Thus the north-south wage differential may also be at least partially attributable to QOL
differences, that is, a preference for living in small cities
or rural areas or simply the socioeconomic region we label
"the south." The migration during the 1970s from Northeast to
South by both whites and blacks, a reversal of the pattern for
several previous decades, would seem to confirm this.

The conclusion we draw from the studies reported here is
that individuals living in smaller cities enjoy a substantially higher QOL (and lower COL) compared to the residents of
larger urban areas. Residents who live in cities of less than
100,000 in general enjoy a higher QOL which adds at least 20
percent to their total real income compared to the residents
of the nation's largest cities.

2. AN APPLICATION OF THE THEORY OF COMPENSATING WAGE DIFFERENTIALS TO THE STATE OF MONTANA

A. Introduction

In order to make the analysis in this and the previous
Chapters more specific, we propose to apply it to one particular area, the State of Montana. Montana is a primarily rural
state with a half dozen small cities in which considerable
manufacturing, mining, and service activity is concentrated.

The State of Montana is in many ways typical of most rural Northern Great Plains states and some of the "high amenity"
Mountain states. For several decades, while its impressive
natural environment has been praised, its "sluggish" or "stag-
gant" economy has been bemoaned by both local government leaders, the business community, and resident economists. The
concern over Montana's economy has focused upon the slow growth
in personal income which combined with migration and birth
rates produced per capita income figures which lagged behind
the national averages.

The discussion in the previous Chapters suggests that
this narrow interpretation of money income in Montana or any
area may be reaching the opposite of the correct conclusions:
The money incomes may be low because people want to live in
Montana to enjoy the amenities of its social and physical environment, and this desire to live in Montana may *force* wages
down to a point where the marginal migrant to Montana is no
better or worse off than (s)he could be elsewhere in the nation.

Before drawing the conclusion that the lower wages in
Montana are not a measure of the lack of health in the economy
but are a measure instead of the higher quality of life, we
must look at the wage differences and migration patterns particular to Montana to be sure that Montana fits the national
pattern. The wage differentials in Montana could be due to
disequilibrium in labor markets in Montana relative to the nation (a surplus work force in Montana) even though similar
differentials across the United States are not due to this
cause.

B. Wage and Income Levels

Almost any measure of wage or money income levels in Montana indicates that wages and incomes in Montana are significantly below the national average.* Table 4.2 lists some of
these measures. Although median family income is only slightly below the national level, a weighted average of wages and
salaries is 22 percent below the national average and per capita personal income is 13 percent below the national average.
The significant difference between these two latter measures
can be traced to the fact that per capita income includes farm
income as well as property (non-wage) income while the weighted average of non-agricultural wages and salaries includes
neither. The ambiguity as to which wage or income measure is
appropriate for our purposes was discussed above. Each has
its own theoretical appeal. Thus we can only say that wages
or money income earning potential in Montana is 5 to 22 percent below the national average. Five seems a low estimate.
Twenty-two seems a bit high. Possibly a 13 percent figure is
a more accurate representation of the "wage differential" we
conceptually wish to measure.

C. Population Growth and Migration

Table 4.3 presents data on changes in Montana's population during the 1960s and 1970s. It is clear that during the
1960s Montana's population growth was far below the national
average and that Montana was exporting people, on net, to
other areas. This would certainly suggest a state labor market lagging behind the natural increase in the state's population. If population adjusted only after some delay one would
except this to cause lower wages. It should be kept in mind,
however, that one reason for a delayed adjustment might be

---

*If one calculates an hourly wage for manufacturing production
workers, one finds that Montana wages were 14 percent *above*
the national average in 1976. This is the only general wage
index which indicates higher incomes in Montana. Statistical
Abstract 1977, p. 414.

Table 4.2

RELATIVE MONEY WAGE AND INCOME LEVELS IN MONTANA

	Montana Average	U.S. Average	Ratio Montana/U.S.
1976 Per capita Personal Income (1)	$ 5,600	$ 6,441	0.87
1975 Median Family Income (2)	$11,516	$12,158	0.95
1973 Average Annual Wages and Salaries in: (3)			
Mining	$11,050	$11,683	0.95
Manufacturing	$ 8,960	$10,027	0.89
Construction	$10,070	$11,277	0.89
Wholesale and Retail Trade	$ 5,880	$ 8,063	0.73
Finance, Insurance, Real Estate	$ 7,200	$ 9,270	0.78
Service	$ 4,920	$ 7,469	0.66
Employment Weighted Average of 1973 Annual Wages and Salaries (4)	$ 7,315	$ 9,378	0.78

Sources: (1) Statistical Abstract 1977, p. 437.

(2) Montana Business Quarterly (Spring 1978): 7.

(3) Montana Data: Montana Business Quarterly (Winter 1975):22.

U.S. Data: Statistical Abstract 1977, p. 413.

(4) Same as (3) using 1974 employment as weights for Montana and 1975 employment as weights for U.S.

Table 4.3

MONTANA POPULATION CHANGES 1960-76 RELATIVE TO THE NATION

	Montana	U.S.
Percent Net Increase in Population 1960-1970 (1)	+2.9%	13.3%
Percent Increase in Population 1970-1976 (2)	+8.4%	5.6%
Net Migration as Percent of Population 1960-1970 (3)	-8.4%	--
Net Migration as Percent of Population 1965-1970 (4)	-5.0%	--
Net Migration as Percent of Population 1970-1976 (5)	÷3.6%	--

Sources: (1) 1960 population base, Statistical Abstract 1977, p. 14.

   (2) 1970 population base, Montana Business Quarterly (Summer 1977): 24; Statistical Abstract 1977, p. 14.

   (3) 1960 population base, Statistical Abstract 1977, p. 14.

   (4) 1970 population base, Montana Business Quarterly (Summer 1975): 6.

that people want to remain in Montana because of the higher QOL. In that situation, part of the wage differential could still be attributed to the differential QOL.

During the 1970s, the pattern of the 1960s appears to

have been reversed.* Montana's population grew 50 percent
faster than the nation's and the state experienced net inmigration. That is, on net, people were migrating to Montana
despite its significantly lower money wages. This fits the
national pattern described above, and is hard to explain in
terms of labor market disequilibrium unless one turns to an
explanation which sees Montana as an attractive place to work
despite the lower money income. The compensating wage differential explanation is exactly that sort of explanation.

D. The Size of Montana's Cities Relative to the Nation's

Table 4.4 gives the distribution of Montana's and the nation's population by size of city. It gives us some feeling
for the character of the urban environment faced by the average Montanan and the average American. The median "size of
place"** when one includes the rural population is 2,500 to
5,000 in Montana and 25,000 to 50,000 in the U.S. Thus there
is an order of magnitude or factor of ten difference.

If we look only at the urban population and form a weighted average of the city size, the average size city in Montana
is 32,000 while the average size city in the U.S. is 502,000.***
Thus there is a 15.7 factor difference or 1.2 orders of magnitude difference (log of 15.7).

---

*Maxine C. Johnson, Director of the Bureau of Business and E-
conomic Research at the University of Montana has suggested
the 1970-1976 population migration data may be inaccurate:
"Population movement is difficult to estimate, however, and
this (population increase figure) may be inaccurate. The figures do show that net immigration slowed considerably between
1975 and 1977. Two years' experience does not make a trend
but it will be interesting to see the figure for the next few
years." Montana Business Quarterly (Spring 1978): 6. However, data contained in the Social Security Administration's
"Continuous Work History" one percent sample indicates that
net migration into Montana *increased* between the 1970-1973
period (2.2%) and the 1973-1976 period (3.6%). This data,
however, excludes agricultural workers and thus partly ignores
what is happening in rural areas. Thus these figures may be
misleading for the state as a whole.

**That is, 50 percent of the population lives in places larger
than this and 50 percent live in places smaller than this.

***In calculating the weighted average, the mid-point in the
city-size range was used except for those cities of over one
million for which three millions was used as the average city
size in the range.

Table 4.4

DISTRIBUTION OF POPULATION BY SIZE OF PLACE, 1970

Percent of Population Living in	Montana %	Cumulative	U.S. %	Cumulative %
Urban areas	53.4	--	73.5	--
cities 1,000,000	0.0	0.0	9.2	9.2
cities 500,000-1,000,000	0.0	0.0	6.4	15.6
cities 250,000-500,000	0.0	0.0	5.1	20.7
cities 100,000-250,000	0.0	0.0	7.0	27.7
cities 50,000-100,000	17.5	17.5	8.2	35.9
cities 25,000-50,000	4.2	21.7	8.8	44.7
cities 10,000-25,000	12.4	34.1	10.5	55.2
cities 5,000-10,000	9.6	43.7	6.4	61.6
cities 2,500-5,000	7.9	51.6	4.0	65.6
cities less than 2,500	--	--	0.4	66.0
unincorporated urban areas	--	53.4	7.5	73.5
Rural areas	46.6	--	26.5	--
rural places 1,000-2,000	7.7	61.1	3.3	76.8
rural places 1,000	0.0	61.1	1.9	78.7
other rural areas	38.9	100.0	21.3	100.0

Source: U.S.: Statistical Abstract 1977, p. 18.

Montana: 1970 Census of the Population, Vol. 1, Part 28, Table 3.

On the basis of the empirical results presented earlier in this Chapter, an order of magnitude difference in size of place is associated with at least a 10 percent difference in wage or money income. Thus if Montana's QOL varies with size of place in a way similar to the national pattern, we would expect wages and money income to be at least 12 percent below the national average. Or, at least twelve percentage points of the lower Montana wage or money income could be explained in terms of differences in the QOL.

5
Direct Measures of the Value of the Quality of Life

1. INTRODUCTION

One criticism of the compensating wage differential approach to estimating the value of the QOL is that it is almost irrefutable and therefore untestable. It assumes individuals move to where their total real income is highest. Therefore if they do not move from low-wage areas like Montana something must be contributing to their total real income which compensates for the lower money wages. We label that hypothesized "something" the higher QOL and are forced by our assumption that individuals move until total real incomes at the margin are identical everywhere in the country to conclude that the compensating flow of environmental values is exactly equal to the difference in wages. The logic here is impeccable but the empirical content very, very low. The argument is built almost entirely upon a pyramid of assumptions. Although most economists may be comfortable with this sort of logical argument, many others may be quite uncomfortable with the scientific standing of the conclusions.

One way of testing the implications of the compensating wage differential theory is to ask whether direct measures of the differential value of parts of an area's environment also suggest an aggregate differential value that offsets the lower wages paid. In this chapter we attempt to answer this question by focusing on four of the most discussed aspects of the QOL in an area, namely crime rates, recreational opportunities, air pollution, and congestion. Although the tools used here have general applicability, to apply them in the abstract would not suggest much about the importance of each and the character of the assumptions necessary to come to quantitative conclusions. Therefore, we again proceed by way of example or case study using the State of Montana as the example of an area asserted by many to have a high quality of life but lagging economy. The quantitative results presented here are only "ball park" estimates with the size of the "ball park" arbitrarily set. They are presented only for illustrative purposes to indicate the advantage and weaknesses of this "direct" alternative approach to the economic value of the QOL.

2. CRIME

One aspect of the quality of life which has been prominent in political debate and discussion during the 1970s has been crime rates. In this area Montanans like most rural and small town populations enjoy a dramatic advantage relative to the rest of the nation. Table 5.1 indicates the crime rates for violent crimes and property crimes for both Montana and the nation.* If one uses these figures to project the risks of being the victim of crime, the data suggests that the risk to Montanans is only about half of what it is to the average American. Yet Montanans spend 35 percent less per person on police protection.** The value of this to Montanans is the \$13.56 per person lower police costs plus the value of increased security and reduced psychic, physical, and material losses. Larger cities spend as much as three times per capita what Montanans do on police protection while maintaining crime rates two to ten times as high.*** This suggests that people are willing to pay through taxes many times what Montanans have to pay even for much lower levels of protection against crime. In addition, individuals in higher crime risk areas privately expend money to reduce the risks through higher insurance premiums, the costs of additional locks, burglar control devices, weapons, and private security guards. Finally, individuals suffer still additional costs associated with increased fear and anxiety and the loss of the use of public places such as parks and city street. If we take the differ-

---

*These "offenses known to police" per 100,000 population grossly understate actual victimization by crime. As many as 3 out of 4 of some violent crimes (e.g., rape) and half of the crimes against property are not reported. However, there appears to be no regional or city size pattern to this underreporting, so it is assumed that no bias is introduced. The President's Commission on Law Enforcement and Administration of Justice, Task Force Report: Crime and Its Impact (Washington, D.C.: Government Printing Office, 1967), p. 28.

**The ratio of 1975 police expenditures to 1976 population was \$38.79 per capita in the U.S. and \$25.23 per capita in Montana. Statistical Abstract, 1977, pp. 28, 180.

***Statistical Abstract, 1977, p. 180.

Table 5.1

CRIME RATES, 1976

(Offenses Known to Police per 100,000 Population)

Offenses	U.S.	Montana	Montana/U.S.
Murder	8.8	5.0	.57
Forcible Rape	26.4	13.5	.51
Robbery	145.8	35.6	.18
Aggravated Assault	229.0	126.0	.55
Burglary	1439.0	841.0	.59
Larceny Theft	2921.0	2933.0	1.00
Motor Vehicle Theft	446.0	308.0	.70

Source: Statistical Abstract, 1977, p. 169.

ence in per capita state and local government expenditures on police between Montana and the U.S. average and double it to account for the fact that police expenditures are, on average, only one-half of the total expenditure on the criminal justice system,* we have the direct savings to Montanans due to lower crime control costs.

In addition to this there is the value of the damage avoided because crime rates are lower. This is a more difficult thing to quantify. We proceed here with a set of assumptions which allow us to use existing data to estimate the willingness to pay for lower crime rates which is implicit in other cities' crime control expenditures. In this we are assuming that Montanans' preferences for crime control are similar to those of other Americans.

Knowing only what cities have been willing to pay to hold crime rates at a particular level is insufficient for estimating the value to those citizens of lower crime rates. Additional assumptions have to be made to fill in the gaps in our knowledge. The basic information we are working with is that in very large cities citizens are willing to pay three times as much per capita as Montanans to hold crime rates at twice the Montana level.

*Ibid., p. 179.

Figure 5.1

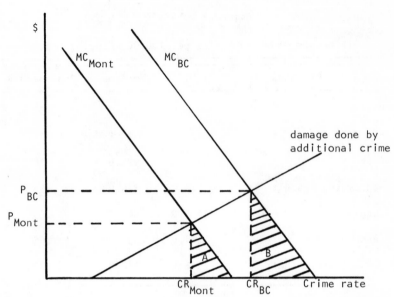

Figure 5.1 indicates how the marginal costs of crime reduction (MC) might interact with the additional damage done by
higher crime rates (the marginal value of crime control) to
determine the price different areas are willing to pay to reduce crime by an additional unit where P_{BC} represents the

price residents of a "Big City" are willing to pay to control
crime and P_{Mont} is the same type of price in Montana where

lower indigenous crime rates do not require as high an expenditure to bring crime rates down to an acceptable level. As
a result Montanans choose to spend less than "big city" residents to control crime.

        For simplicity we assume linear marginal crime control
and crime damage cost relationships and assume that the lower
level of social control in larger cities is completely reflected by the higher marginal costs of crime control at any
given level of crime, that is, by a vertical shift in the marginal cost of crime control curve. Both of these assumptions
are arbitrary and abandoning them for equally plausible assumptions could significantly affect the results.

        Area A and B under the MC curves are the total expendi-
tures on crime control in Montana and in a large city (approximately $50 per capita and $150 per capita).* The difference
between them is part of the advantage Montanans enjoy. The

*See above text. The figures for "large cities" represents
the largest cities in the U.S. Statistical Appendix 1977, p. 180.

other part of the advantage is the value of the lower crime
rates shown as the area under the marginal damage curve in
Figure 5.2, abcd.

Figure 5.2

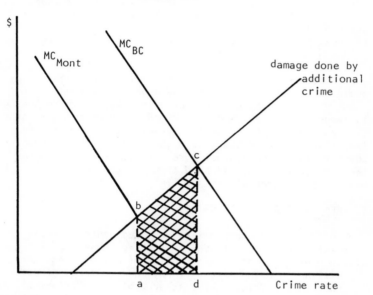

To estimate this area we need to know what price Montanans and
residents of large cities would be willing to pay to reduce
crime rates by an additional unit. We could possibly obtain
this by studying the relationship between cities' crime bud-
gets and crime rates, but do not now know this. Thus we fill
in with additional assumptions. The point where the MC curves
intercept the crime rate ("X") axis is the level of crime
which would exist if there were no state and local government
crime control. If we arbitrarily assume that total gross
crime rates would double if only private and federal crime
control continued at current expenditure levels, we can use
the total expenditures to estimate the price citizens are
willing to pay to reduce crime rates by one unit. The assumed increase in crime rates without state and local control
is represented by the base of triangles A and B in Figure 5.1
and the total expenditure is the area of those triangles.
Thus, using the formula for the area of a triangle, we can
estimate the height of the triangles. This is the marginal
value or marginal cost (they are equal) of crime control; i.e.,
the heights ab and cd in Figure 5.2. These come out to be
3.0 cents per capita per unit reduction in crime rate in the
U.S. and 2.0 cents per capita in Montana. We now can combine

this information with the difference in crime rates in the U.S. (the base of the trapazoid abcd in Figure 5.2) to estimate the value of lower crime rates in Montana, the area abcd. This comes out to $125.00 per capita. This combined with the $27.00 per capita benefit of lower crime control expenditures (two times the $13.56 mentioned above) comes to over $150.00 per capita or a total for the State of Montana of $112,950,000 per year for the value of this aspect of the quality of life in Montana.

This seems to be a reasonable "ball park" figure, if one asks whether Montanans would pay thirty-three cents a day to avoid the insecurity much of the urban population of this country faces because of higher crime rates. Those Americans in large urban areas who can afford it spend far more than $125 per person to reduce the impact of crime on themselves. They live in more distant or higher rent neighborhoods; they buy more insurance and pay more for it; they hire doormen and security guards; install burglar alarms, etc. and pay high medical bills when all this fails.

3. RECREATIONAL OPPORTUNITIES

Almost all Montanans like most residents of rural areas live within an hour's travel of fishing, hunting, hiking, pleasure driving, etc., the quality of which other Americans are willing to spend literally days and hundreds of dollars to experience. This is demonstrated by the millions of visitors from across the nation who visit Glacier and Yellowstone National Parks, Montana's wilderness areas, and Montana's "blue ribbon trout streams" as well as the thousands who buy out-of-state fishing and hunting permits at a cost many times what Montanans have to pay. Montanans enjoy a relative advantage in two ways: access to these recreational resources is less costly in terms of both time and money than it is to the typical American seeking similar recreational opportunities and the quality of the recreational resources is higher. Montanans respond to these advantages, as an economist would except, by participating more in outdoor recreation. As indicated in Table 5.2, the participation rates in outdoor recreational activity in Montana are two to four times as high as the national average.

Figure 5.3 graphically indicates the gross advantage Montanans enjoy. We assume linear demand curves with the demand curve for Montana's recreational opportunities lying above that for the average recreational opportunities in the United States by a vertical amount representing the value of the superior quality of Montana's recreational resources. Implicitly, this assumes that people would pay, if they had to, ab more to enjoy recreational opportunities of the quality available in Montana compared to what they would pay for the experience of average quality in the United States. We draw

Table 5.2

PARTICIPATION RATES IN OUTDOOR RECREATION

(% of the Population Participating)

Activity	Montana Rate (1966-68)	U.S. Rate (1965)	Montana Rate / U.S. Rate
Fishing	41.6	21.9	1.9
Hunting	24.8	8.8	2.8
Camping	27.1	7.3	3.7
Skiing	9.2	2.9	3.2

Source: U.S. data: Statistical Abstract, 1970, Table 306.
Montana data: Montana Statewide Outdoor Recreation
Plan, Montana Department of Fish and Game, Appendix
A, Table A-4, 1969. Both sets of data are of doubtful accuracy based as they are on survey techniques
which may not involve random sampling of the population. A more careful random survey of U.S. households by the Bureau of Outdoor Recreation in the summer of 1972 showed similar differences between western states and the U.S. average with westerners almost twice as likely to engage in camping, backpacking, etc. Hunting and skiing were not covered
because the survey focused on summer outdoor recreation. Participation in fishing was only 11 percent
higher in the west. See Outdoor Recreation: A
Legacy for America, BOR, 1973, Tables 1-5 and 2-2.

the current costs of participating (time, travel costs, etc.)
in Montana, C_m, below the cost of participating in similar
activities faced by other Americans. The net value gained by
participation is then the triangle C ad for the average American and C_m be for a Montanan. If, in ^{us} this situation, Montanans
engage in twice as much outdoor recreation, $Q_m = 2Q_{us}$, then
using similar triangle relationships, the area of the Montana
triangle, the net benefits to Montanans, are four times as
great as those to the average American because similar

66

Figure 5.3

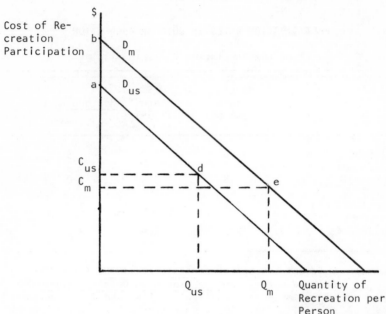

triangles assure us that $C_m b = 2C_{us} a$.* Thus, given these assumptions, Montanans are four times better off than the average American when it comes to these particular recreational
opportunities. This does not put a dollar value on this advantage. To do this we need to know the number of person days
per capita of each particular type of recreational experience
in the U.S. and the average value of those experiences. Table
5.3 provides this information. Multiplying the days per capita and value per day and summing over the four activities
listed, we get $32.41 per capita. Multiplying this by a fac-
tor of 4, we get the higher value to Montanans, $129.64 per

*The relationship implied here can be made explicit in the
following way: If the cost at which all demand for the recreational experiences ceases is 5 times the current price, then,
for instance, a quality differential of 50% and cost differential of 75% would give this result, or a quality differential of 75% and cost differential of 12%. If the cost at
which all demand ceases is two times the current cost, a 20%
quality and 30% cost differential would yield this result.

Table 5.3

RECREATION DAYS PER CAPITA AND RECREATION VALUES PER DAY

Activity	participation rate (1)*	days per participant (2)*	days per capita (1) X (2)	average value**
Fishing	.24	7.3	1.75	3.78
Hunting	.14	13.5	1.89	7.55
Camping remote area	.05	7.5	0.38	7.55
developed area	.11	8.8	0.97	6.04
Skiing	.05	8.1	0.41	6.80

*Statistical Abstract, 1977, p. 231, year is 1972.

**Water Resources Council values multiplied by 1.51 to convert to 1978 dollars. Federal Register, Vo. 36, No. 245, December 21, 1971.

capita. The difference, $97.23 per capita, is the advantage Montanans enjoy just from these four selected activities. Snowmobiling, hiking, photography, picnicking, pleasure driving, four-wheel drive exploration, bicycling, rock hounding, mountaineering, river rafting, etc., should be added to the list. This would certainly double the above figure giving us a total gross differential benefit to Montanans of approximately $200 per capita or $150,600,000 per year for all Montanans.

Montanans, of course, are at a disadvantage when it comes to other types of outdoor recreation. For instance, they have almost no possibility of attending professional sports events or participating in deep-sea or warm water fishing. Thus people living near recreational opportunities to which Montanans have limited access or access only to lower quality opportunities have an advantage relative to Montanans. We make no attempt to net out these disadvantages of living in Montana. Thus the whole discussion here is in terms of the *gross* advantage Montanans have because of the superior recreational opportunities available in Montana for the listed recreational activities.

If one were to take into account the fact that individuals actively try to develop tastes and abilities which allow them to enjoy what superior recreational opportunities are readily available where they live, the problem becomes even more complex for one of the primary concepts economists depend upon, fixed tastes, has to be abandoned. A realistic investigation on Montanans' relative advantage might well have to take these "adjusted tastes" into account. The impact of this would cut both ways: In all locations people would tend to "like what they had" and so differences in welfare would be reduced. On the other hand, changes in the environment which threatened resources which the population had become dependent upon would be more costly in terms of their impact on individual welfare.

4. AIR POLLUTION

Most Montanans, as most small city and rural residents, enjoy significantly higher air quality than the average American. This lengthens life expectancy, reduces sickness, improves the aesthetic character of the "big sky," and saves on cleaning costs, painting, replacement of corroded materials, etc.* Thus there are both psychic (less pain, longer life, and clearer vistas) and more traditionally "economic" costs (lost earnings, medical expenditures, repair and cleaning) avoided by living in areas such as Montana.

Many Montana cities have surprisingly high pollution levels and given the small size of those cities, the levels of pollution are all the more startling. However, despite the high sulfur dioxide levels in Laurel, East Helena, and Anaconda and the high particulate levels in Missoula, Columbia Falls and Great Falls, most Montanans breath air which is substantially cleaner than the national average.** Table 5.4 presents average annual pollution levels in major Montana cities. If we weight the 1977 air quality data in each city reporting by the city's population, accepting the high-level reporting station in the central city as representative of the whole city when a city-wide average was not available, the average particulate pollution level is 57.91 micrograms per cubic meter for the 35 percent of the state's population in these cities. The average level of SO_2 pollution is 6.28 micrograms per cubic meter for that same fraction of the population. If we assume the other 65 percent of the population faces particulate pollution one-quarter of the national average (1/4 of 60 micrograms per cubic meter) and almost zero sulfur dioxide pollution, the average levels for the whole state are 30 micrograms of particulate per cubic meter and 6.3 micrograms of SO_2 per cubic meter. The average U.S. levels in 1975 were 60 micrograms of particulate per cubic meter and 20 micrograms of

*For a review of the literature on pollution damage costs, see Lester B. Lave and Eugene P. Seskin, Air Pollution and Human Health, Resources for the Future (Baltimore: Johns Hopkins University Press, 1977), Chapter 10.

**See Annual Air Quality Data Summary for Montana, 1977, Air Quality Bureau, Montana Department of Health and Environmental Sciences, May 1978.

Table 5.4

1977 ANNUAL AVERAGE POLLUTION LEVELS
(micrograms per cubic meter)

City	Particulate	Sulfur Dioxide
Billings	47.7	5.33
Great Falls	88.8	--
East Helena	66.7	80.00
Anaconda	43.9	67.00
Miles City	15.5	--
Broadus	14.4	--
Glendive	19.1	--
Missoula	82.8	--
Columbia Falls	92.9	--
Libby	42.6	--
Helena	--	16.00
Butte	92.7	--
Bozeman	--	--
Weighted Average of these cities	57.91	6.82
U.S. Average	60.00	20.00

Source: Pollution Levels: Air Quality Bureau, Montana
         Department of Health and Environmental Sciences,
         Annual Air Quality Data Summary, 1977.

SO_2 per cubic meter.* Those averages are for areas where 80 percent of the U.S. population lives. If we make the same assumptions about the rural non-reporting areas in the U.S. that we made for Montana, these averages become 51 and 16 micrograms per cubic meter of particulate and SO_2 respectively. Thus Montana's average level of particulate pollution is 40 percent below the national average and its average level of SO_2 is 60 percent below the national average.**

Lave and Seskin*** have estimated the impact on mortality of various levels of sulfur and particulate pollution. They find no level below which these two pollutants have no impact on health and thus use a linear function to estimate the impact of reductions of pollution as high as 82 percent of the 1970 levels. If we apply their pollution-mortality elasticities**** for particulates and SO_2 to estimate the impact of 40 percent lower particulate and 60 percent lower SO_2, we obtain a 5 percent reduction in the mortality rate. Lave and Seskin estimate the dollar value of a 7 percent reduction in mortality rate. If we convert this to a per capita figure and take five-sevenths of it, the value of the lower pollution levels in Montana (just due to a reduction in health related costs) is $84.00 per capita in 1978 dollars.*****

Lave and Seskin take a very narrow view of the health-related costs: the lost income and increased medical expenditures associated with higher morbidity and shorter lives. Thaler and Rosen,****** using methods similar to those used in this paper to estimate the value of the QOL, studied the higher wage rates which must be paid to workers to get them to work at jobs with higher injury and death rates. This is the minimum

---

*EPA, Trends in the Quality of the Nation's Air, March 1977, pp. 5-7.

**The Montana data (and no doubt the U.S. data too) is of questionable reliability. Monitoring stations are not always placed rationally and adjacent stations sometimes report quite different results. In addition, there are wide variations over time in any given location. At best these averages are only suggestive of the differences with the national averages.

***Op. cit., p. 226.

****Ibid., equation 8.5-7, p. 176.

*****Calculations based on data in Lave and Seskin, op.cit., pp. 223-227.

******R. Thaler and S. Rosen, "The Value of Saving a Life: Evidence from the Labor Market" in N. Terleckyj, ed., Household Production and Consumption, NBER, 1976, p. 265.

amount of compensation workers need before they will accept
the increased risk and thus can be taken as a measure of the
value to workers of safer jobs, and a longer, more healthy
life. Gregor has used their estimates of the value of reduced health risks to estimate the value of air quality improvements in the Pittsburgh area.* He estimates that each 1 percent decrease in pollution levels if worth $5 per capita for
particulate pollution and 36 cents per capita for SO_2 pollution. For the decreases we have used, 40 and 60 percent, this
would be $200 and $21 per capita or a total of $221 per capita.
Both Gregor and Thaler and Rosen get significantly higher figures than the loss-of-earnings based figures. This would be
expected given that pain, sickness, and early death are avoided for reasons other than the lower lifetime earnings they
cause.

    Michelson and Tourin estimated in 1966 that cleaning and
repair costs in heavily polluted cities result in $84.00 per
capita higher costs than what were faced in a relatively un-
polluted one. If we use only 25 percent of this and convert
it to 1978 dollars, we would get an additional $42.00 per cap-
ita saved in Montana as a result of lower pollution levels.

    To these benefits should be added the value of the clear-
er vistas and other aesthetic aspects. From them should be
subtracted the costs associated with air pollutants common to
some Montana towns but unusual elsewhere in the country (hy-
drygen sulfide, fluorides, heavy metals, etc.).

    The above suggests that Montanans, because of lower pol-
lution levels, enjoy a $125.00 to $263.00 advantage per capita
relative to the rest of the nation. This is a total annual
value of $94 to $198 million dollars for the whole state.

5. TRAVEL TIME AND CONGESTION

    As the size of a city increases, larger distances must be
traveled to reach work, do errands, etc. The additional cost
can be avoided by living in a more central location, but this
will involve higher rents and/or other social and environmental drawbacks. Tables 5.5 and 5.6 provide some data on work
trip length and duration by size of city. Note that both distance and travel time increase with city size. If we use

---

*John J. Gregor, "Intra-Urban Mortality and Air Quality: An
Economic Analysis of the Costs of Pollution Induced Mortality,"
Center for the Study of Policy, Penn State University, 1977.

**I. Michelson and B. Tourin, "Comparative Methods of Studying
the Costs of Controlling Air Pollution," Public Health Reports,
Vol. 81, p. 505.

Table 5.5

ESTIMATED AVERAGE WORK TRIP LENGTH AND DURATION

FOR AUTOMOBILE DRIVERS (one-way trip)

Size of Urban Area	Number of Cities in Sample	Trip Length Miles	Trip Time Minutes
10,000 - 100,000	4	3	6.4
100,000 - 1,000,000	13	5	10.5
above 1,000,000	6	6.2	15.9

Source: Alan M. Voorhees et al., "Factors in Work-trip Lengths,"
Highway Research Record 14 (1966):24-26. Cited in
Irving Hoch, "Income and City Size," op. cit.

Table 5.6

TIME SPENT BY HEADS OF FAMILIES IN DAILY

WORK TRIPS BY LOCATION

(roundtrip, minutes per day)

	New York-N.J. Consolidated Area	Next largest 12 SMSA's		Other SMSA's		Outside SMSA's	
		central city	suburb	central	suburb	adjacent	outlying
Median time	63	53	50	35	41	27	17
Average time	68	59	55	42	43	42	25

Source: James N. Morgan et al., Productive Americans (Ann
Arbor: University of Michigan, Institute of Social
Research, 1966), Survey Research Monograph 43, Table
S-3, p. 80. Cited in Irving Hoch, "Income and City
Size," op. cit.

Beesley's* and Hoch's** evidence on how people evaluate time
lost traveling and evaluate travel time at one-third the wage
rate, both the quantity of time and the cost per unit time will
increase with city size because wages increase with city size.
Hoch's rough calculations*** using data in Table 5.6 leads to
an estimate that individuals living outside of large cities
(SMSA's) (as do 76 percent of Montana's population)**** save
about 4 percent of their income in travel costs compared to
individuals living in the New York-New Jersey consolidated
metropolitan area. Thus just taking into account travel time
to work (and ignoring other travel time), wages in that area
would have to be 4 percent higher just to make individuals as
well off as individuals living outside of the nation's largest
cities.

　　For the half of Montana's population living in or near
urban areas, the above information is probably relevant. Their
travel times to work etc. are quite short.***** Four percent of
Montana per capita income would be $224 per capita in 1976.
For the other half of Montanans living in rural areas, travel
times to work may still be quite short for many live on farms
where they work. However, travel time to shop and entertainment and off-farm jobs may be quite long. The isolation and
huge size of Montana may make travel costs for this part of
the population substantial.

6.　SUMMARY

　　Table 5.7 summarizes the results of our attempt to look
directly at the value to Montanans of specific aspects of the
QOL in Montana. The total for just these four characteristics
is $834 per capita or 15 percent of the 1976 per capita money
income in Montana. The implication is, that even if per capita

---

*M.E. Beesley, "The Value of Time Spent Travelling: New Evi-
dence," Economica, May 1965.

**Irving Hoch, "Income and City Size," op. cit., p. 316.

***Ibid., p. 317.

****Only Great Falls and Billings are SMSA's. The entire
county population was used as the SMSA population.

*****Data on travel time to work which is specific to Montana
is not available. If fact the closest regional data is for
all of the Western states. Thus that data lumps together California and Montana. Both Great Falls and Los Angeles fall
into the same SMSA category. That data does indicate that
westerners have somewhat shorter travel times to work. See
Current Housing Reports, Series H 150-75, 1970, pp. 7 and 155.

Table 5.7

VALUE OF PARTICULAR ASPECTS OF MONTANA'S QOL

COMPARED TO THE U.S. AVERAGE

Quality	Per Capita Value	Total Value to Population
Lower crime rate	$150	$112,950,000
Cheaper Access to High Quality Recreation	200	150,600,000
Cleaner Air	260	195,000,000
Reduced Travel Time to Work*	224	84,000,000
TOTAL	834	$518,550,000

*These values are relative to urban residents in very large cities *not* relative to the U.S. average. It is assumed to apply to only one-half of the Montana population.

money income in Montana were 15 percent below the national average (which it is not; it was 13 percent below the national average in 1977), Montanans' total real income per capita would not be any lower than the national average. The value of these four advantages living in Montana would have compensated them for the lower money income.

In interpreting these results two important considerations must be kept in mind: 1) The numbers and values are offered only to suggest the relative size the value of these QOL might have. No attempt at an accurate estimation of these values has been attempted. The point was to suggest the relative order of magnitude, i.e. one-tenth of one percent, one percent, ten percent, etc. Each estimate is easily open to challenge. They are "back-of-the-envelope" estimates whose usefulness is limited to their illustrative purpose. 2) Only four "qualities of life" in Montana have been discussed and only very limited aspects of each of these. Thus many valuable qualities have been ignored. Similarly, any negative features of living in Montana other than lower money income have been ignored.

7. OTHER DIRECT MEASURES OF THE RELATIVE QUALITY OF LIFE

Starting in the 1960s both economists and geographers have shown an interest in geographic variations in various indices of social well-being. Dissatisfied with such measures as per capita income, median family income, rate of economic growth, unemployment rate, etc., even as measures of the health of the economy not to mention overall social well-being, they have tried to combine available data on a wide variety of socioeconomic characteristics to create very broad indicators of the "quality of life" in various areas. We thus have a variety of direct measures of social well-being relative to the rest of the nation to compare with our reading of the wage differentials. However, unlike wage differentials and the aspects of the QOL discussed previously in this Chapter, these indices do not attempt to put a dollar value or any value on the level of well-being measured. They simply establish index numbers which indicate how far from the national mean or median various states or cities are.

Also, it should be kept in mind that most of these indices are "data driven," that is, the availability of consistent data on each state or each city was a primary determinant of whether a particular quality was included in the index or not. For instance, for smaller SMSA's, such as Great Falls and Billings, Montana, there is not a ready source of air pollution and water pollution data on a uniform reporting basis. Thus in some measures of these smaller cities' environmental quality, air and water pollution are ignored and acres of parks are used instead! While this may be appropriate in comparing large cities, it is *silly in* largely rural states. Thus theory and logic do not always guide the content of the indices; ease of data collection does.

Finally, when combining data on different aspects of a region, some weighting scheme must be used. Previously in this study we have used dollar weights; however, these other studies, as mentioned above, do not. This creates problems. In measuring social stability, for instance, should all crimes be weighed the same or should violent crimes count more heavily than property crimes or crimes of consumption (e.g., drug use)? Should divorce rates count equally with crime in measuring social stability or not count at all? Etc. Most of the indices presented below implicitly weight each factor in a similar category equally. This is done because there is no general agreement on the relative importance of various qualities of life. But most of these studies also test the relative rankings of areas' QOL for sensitivity to different weightings. The results usually have been that the relative rankings do not change significantly. Of course, very dramatic changes in weighting would have a significant effect.

In the following tables several sets of these social indices are presented. Montana is again used as a particular

case in point. These indices indicate, in general, that while
Montana's lagging economy in the late 1950s led to indices of
economic well being which placed the state well below the national median and/or average, the indicators of other aspects
of social well being during that same period placed Montana
well above the national median. Indicators constructed around
a 1970 data base show that even in terms of broad economic
health, despite the implications of the more narrow per capita income figures cited earlier, Montana's performance was
either average or slightly above average while indices of
other qualities of Montana life were far above average. Liu's
rankings, for instance, place Montana 9th in the overall index
of QOL despite its simultaneous ranking of 35th in the narrow
economic indicator "per capita income." His rankings of Montana's two SMSAs, Great Falls and Billings, are also high despite some biases in the data against small cities located in
largely rural areas.

For several of the sets of indicators, narrow measures of
economic well being and qualities of life indicators diverge
substantially. Those states with the most "developed" economies and highest ratings in terms of income per capita have
the worst ratings in terms of social pathology, environmental
quality, political participation, etc. Thus there appears to
be a tradeoff between higher income and other qualities of
life. Our theoretical argument above about compensating wage
differentials would lead us to expect this result. It should
be pointed out, however, that according to these indices, per
capita income is not a good measure of even economic health.
The correlation between this and other narrow economic indicators and the indices of economic health used, for instance, by
Liu are very low. Thus, although wages and income may be
traded for a quality environment, economic health need not.

An Appendix to this Book lists the variables which various analysts have used to construct their indices. Only by
reviewing these does one get a feeling for both the breadth
limitations, and arbitrariness of these indices.

Table 5.8

LIU's INDICES OF THE QUALITY OF LIFE IN MONTANA, 1970

Name of Index	Montana's Score (U.S. Average = 1.00)	Standard Deviation Among States
Individual States	1.15	0.16
Equality	1.15	0.19
Living Conditions	1.03	0.19
Agriculture	1.35	0.31
Technology	0.80	0.42
Economic Status	1.07	0.29
Education	1.43	0.26
Health and Welfare	1.13	0.15
State & Local Government	1.23	0.18
Overall QOL	1.15	0.17

Note: Montana ranks 9th in the overall ratings while ranking 35th in p.c. income. This is the largest gap in these two rankings of any state.

Source: Ben C. Liu, "Variations in the Quality of Life in the United States by State, 1970," Review of Social Economy 32, no. 2 (October 1974): 140.

Table 5.9

WILSON'S QOL RANKINGS, 1960-65

Indicator	Montana's Rank (1 is highest 50 is lowest)
Individual Status	19th
Racial Equality	--
Education	25th
Economic Growth Quality	46th
Technological Change	47th
Agriculture	5th
Living Conditions	23rd
Health & Welfare	19th

Source: Environmental Protection Agency, The QOL Concept, op. cit., pp. 11-279.

Table 5.10

SMITH'S MEASURES OF SOCIAL WELL BEING FOR MONTANA

WHEN ALL VARIABLES ARE WEIGHTED EQUALLY

Index Name	Index Value U.S. Average Score = 0, Standard Deviation = 1
Income, Wealth & Employment	0.13
Housing Environment	0.21
Health	-0.27
Education	0.43
Social Disorganization	0.71
Alienation	-0.19
General Social Well Being	0.27

Source: David M. Smith, The Geography of Social Well Being in the U.S., New York, McGraw-Hill, 1973, p. 87

Table 5.11

SMITH'S RANKING OF MONTANA WHEN PRINCIPAL COMPONENT

ANALYSIS IS USED TO ASSIGN WEIGHTS

Index Name	Montana Rank
1. General Socioeconomic Well Being	25th
2. Social Pathology	9th
3. Mental Health	12th
4. Sum of Scores on 1 and 2	16th

Source: David M. Smith, The Geography of Social Well Being in the U.S., New York, McGraw-Hill, 1973, p. 96.

Table 5.12

LIU's QUALITY OF LIFE INDICES FOR GREAT FALLS AND BILLINGS,

COMPARED TO THE 95 SMALLEST SMSA's, 1970

Index	Billings		Great Falls	
	Rank	Rating	Rank	Rating
Economic Component	50 in 95	good	83 in 95	substandard
Political Component	18 in 95	outstanding	59 in 95	good
Environmental Component	82 in 95	substandard	22 in 95	excellent
Health and Education Component	15 in 95	outstanding	22 in 95	excellent
Social Component	6 in 95	outstanding	27 in 95	excellent
Overall QOL	15 in 95	excellent	49 in 95	good

Source: B.C. Liu, Quality of Life Indicators in U.S. Metropolitan Areas, 1970, op. cit., Chapter VII.

6
Values, Economic Values, and the Limits of Economic Analysis

1. INTRODUCTION

In the preceeding Chapters we have crudely measured the value of regional differences in the quality of life. As a result of that analysis, we have shown that the value of the different mix of services flowing from the physical and social environment in different areas can add as much as fifty percent to individuals' real total income. That is the extreme: the difference between a large northeastern congested and polluted city with serious crime problems and a small city in a high amenity rural area in the West. In general we have established that the value of the differences in QOL among areas is substantial. The question we wish to deal with in this chapter is just what economists mean when they assert that the value of the differences in the QOL between two areas is, say, $1500 per capita per year.

As emphasized in the first Chapter, this does *not* mean that economists are saying that according to their own personal judgement that is what the differences in the QOL are worth. The economists are *not* the ones assigning the value. Economists study the behavior of groups of people to try to discover the relative values implicit in those peoples' behavior. Economists are trying to see what value groups of people place on various goods and services by studying those peoples' behavior with respect to those goods and services. In that sense, economists are trying to make explicit the values implicit in peoples' observable behavior. The relative value economists try to come up with, then, is an estimate of the value that various people in fact assign to that good or service themselves. Economists tend to use theoretical analysis and behavioral observation to determine peoples' personal valuations instead of directly asking individuals how they value a particular service or resource because economists have doubts about the accuracy of such off-the-top-of-the-head verbal statements. Actual, real world choices in the use of re-

81

sources are taken as a better indicator of peoples' relative
valuation than responses to hypothetical questions where in-
accuracy or mistatement has no consequences to the people involved.

In short, economists assume that there is some logic to
our actions with respect to the resources, goods, and services
we use and that the study of that action will reveal that logic and thereby the relative value we individually and collectively associate with those resources.

Many will object that while this is a legitimate scientific method in studying market behavior, it is of questionable
use once one moves out of the commercial world. Economics,
it will be argued by some, can only deal with commercial or
market values. Aesthetic values, social values, religious values, cultural values, political values, etc. are totally outside the domain of economics and the analysis in the previous
Chapters ignores these narrow limits on the type of value or
values to which economics is applicable. Thus, these people
would argue, the QOL or the environment must be looked upon
as primarily aesthetic, social, cultural, or political not as
economic. And for that reason it has to be analyzed with different tools. It is with that concern that this Chapter deals.

2. ECONOMIC AND NON-ECONOMIC VALUES: IS THERE A DISTINCTION?

A casual consideration of "aesthetic" values will indicate that the distinction between types of value on which the
above objection centers is not very tenable.

Aesthetic considerations are not exclusively or even particularly limited to the natural environment. The construction of the human-made environment is often dominated by aesthetic considerations. That is what architecture, interior
decorating, and landscape architecture are all about. Yet
these are clearly commercial activities which few would dis-
pute could be the subject of economic analysis.

Although these aesthetic considerations are often "intangible" such as the "atmosphere" which is created, this has not
kept designers and buyers from entering into contractual arrangements for the creation of that intangible "atmosphere."
Fancy restaurants and dinner clubs sell primarily an "atmosphere." Restaurant goers seem to be perfectly capable of dis-
tinguishing the differences in the aesthetic characteristics
of both the good and the atmosphere and of deciding how much
they are willing to pay to obtain them. The same can be said
of the services of interior decorators, etc.

There is a market for art work, music, poetry, etc.
Prices do get attached to these "products" even though many of
us may feel the compensation to the artist is often too low.
In fact, economists have put some effort into the study of the
economics of the performing arts and explaining why the arts

tend to face regular financial crises.*

Given the important role that aesthetics play in many clearly commercial activities, given that individuals regularly estimate what it is worth to them to pursue aesthetic objectives, and given that economists have for some time helped analyze the arts, why should environmental values be excluded from economic analysis? Why is the value of an exclusive restaurant's "atmosphere" calculable but not the value of a bucolic natural setting? What is it that allows the value of a quiet suburban neighborhood with its broad green lawns, abundant foliage, and unobtrusive single story houses to be measured but not the value of wildlands or natural parks?

This line of argument is not limited only to aesthetic values. Similar points could be made about "cultural" or "social" values. The value of a worker in most enterprises does not depend solely on hours of work effort. Social and cultural values such as initiative, responsibility, ability to get along with others, punctuality etc. are crucial, and personnel officers seek people with these social and cultural values. Similarly, any progressive economy depends upon the entrepenurial or enterprising spirit of its leaders. "Labor" input into the economy is not just a matter of worker-hours or calories of muscle energy or some other "objective" economic factor. Labor productivity is strongly tied to cultural and social values. Personnel officers are not frustrated or baffled by this. They still can evaluate job applicants and estimate affordable wages and salaries. Our school systems and job retraining programs realize the economic value of these cultural and social values and try to develop and pass them on to their students and clients. Again the "social" and "cultural" nature of the problem does not make it "non-economic" and outside the realm of economics.

Finally, most commodities bought and sold in the commercial market place are not homogeneous products with a single dimensioned use-value which leads people to want them. Most of those products carry with them significant cultural or social attributes which are as important to the purchasers as the "use value." We do not just buy utilitarian and automotive transportation, clothes, food, or "recreational" drugs. An entire multi-billion dollar a year industry has developed which aims at endowing products with social and cultural meaning. We call it "advertising" or "product differentiation," but what it attempts to do is associate some cultural or social value with a product so as to make it more valuable. Although the particular commercial form this mingling of cultural and material values has taken is unusual (and, to some, disgusting), the mingling of these utilitarian values with

---

*William J. Baumol and William G. Bowen, <u>Performing Arts: The Economic Dilemma</u>, Twentieth Century Fund, N.Y. 1966.

other values is not unusual in human history. In almost all
societies tools, ways of producing, food, drugs and dress had
religious, cultural, and social meaning as well as the obvious
utilitarian function. This mingling of values has rarely made
it impossible to put a value on the products involved. In our
society as well as many other societies, this mixing of values
has not prevented exchange, trade, or marketing of the product. People have in fact been able to determine how valuable
the product was to them.

None of the above is meant to suggest that there is nothing unusual about environmental resources which makes their
evaluation particularly difficult. There are many things
which make the determination of such values very, very difficult and possibly impossible given the current state of economic analysis and the type of data available. Further, the
mingling of various qualities in a single good or service
which allows it to satisfy several needs simultaneously does
raise serious conceptual problems for conventional analysis.
The point we have been trying to make, however, is that the
mere presence of aesthetic, cultural, or social considerations
does not indicate that economic analysis is either in prin-
ciple inappropriate or conceptually impossible.

The primary difficulty faced when trying to establish the
value of environmental resources is not, then, the difficulty
individuals have in establishing what that value is to themselves, but the difficulty an outside observer like the economic analyst has in determining what value judgement the individual has in fact made. In a market setting an explicit observable, quantitative act is engaged in (the purchase of a
quantity of the good for a certain amount of money) by the individual which provides some preliminary if somewhat flawed
data with which to start. When no market exists for the resource, good, or service being analyzed, the economist has
little with which to start. The previous Chapters have indicated several crude tools the economist does have available in
this situation to try to estimate the value individuals associate with environmental services. However, much additional
work, both theoretical and empirical, is needed before we can
attain the degree of accuracy which would make public decision
makers comfortable.

3. A DEFINITION OF "VALUE" ACCEPTABLE TO
    BOTH PHILOSOPHER AND ECONOMIST.

For almost a hundred pages we have been using the term
"value" without providing a definition of it. In the empirical and theoretical analysis of previous Chapters we depended
upon the common language meaning of the word: the relative importance of something to people. Although this was sufficient
in order to proceed originally, it may not be sufficient to
resolve the doubts readers may have as to exactly what the

economist is doing and saying. There may be a lingering sus-
picion or a very explicit doubt about whether the analysis we
have been through in this book was not built on the economist's
misuse of terms borrowed from other disciplines. If that were
the case, the analysis and its conclusions might be built a-
round a confusing play on words: the use of a concept, value,
which is common to both philosophy and economics, in a way
that blurs important differences in the way the two fields use
the word. We will argue that this is not the case.

The economist distinguishes between the *values* held by a
person and the *value* of things. Economists deal hardly at all
with the values of individuals and societies. In economics,
vague references to "preference," "tastes," "wants," or
"needs" are made in describing an existing set of values of
unexplored origin which determine or influence how individuals
and groups act with respect to resources. The social psychological processes which produce and change these values are
largely ignored by economists as they focus on the rational
behavior they assume those values guide. What economists seek
to determine is not those underlying values but the *relative
value* human action indicates people attach to various goods
and services. This relative value is certainly assumed to be
tied to basic values, but the economist does not pursue that
connection very far.

For a definition of "value," economists can easily live
with the definition offered by Philosopher Kurt Baier in his
"What is Value? An Analysis of the Concept."* The value of
something is its "capacity to confer a benefit on someone, to
make a favorable difference to his life. The magnitude of its
value is the measure of that capacity."

Knowledge of the value of things, accoring to Baier, is
basic to rational action: "Value assessments tell us which
things have this capacity [to confer benefits on people] in a
higher and which in a lower degree....[S]uch knowledge enables
us to make rational choices *between* things all of which have
this capacity, and all of which are therefore capable of con-
ferring *some* benefit on us....knowledge of the value of things
will be relevant, not to say indispensable, to anyone who
wants to know what he should do. For such knowledge tells him
what contributions towards the improvement of his life he may
expect from the alternatives open to him.**

Baier explicitly includes the "quality of life" as contributing to the value people can receive: "Another way of
increasing a person's ability to make favorable differences to
his life is to improve what might be called *the quality of
life*. I have in mind the natural and cultural *amenities*, the
variety and quality of the goods and services made available

Values and the Future, Kurt Baier and Nicholas Rescher, eds.,
The Free Press, New York, 1969, p. 40.
**Ibid, pp. 48 and 50.

to the members of a given society.*

This definition of value *is* the meaning economists give the concept. Yet economists have often been charged with knowing the "price of everything but value of none." Two explanations of this charge are relevant here. As pointed out earlier, economists have in the past concentrated on market or commercial values while ignoring non-market but very real and important values. This is a major failure and an important and persistent bias which this study has tried to help eliminate. Secondly, economists focus primarily on goods and services which are reproducible or at least are available in relatively abundant supply and then they focus on value "at the margin," i.e. on the value of small changes in availability. That is, economists do not deal with "ultimate" value questions like "What is the value of human life?" or "What is the value of Bald Eagles?" Instead they ask "What is the value of reducing the probability of death by five hundreths of one percent?" or "What is the value of preventing a ten percent decline in the Bald Eagle population?" Irreplaceable, one-of-a-kind, resources present valuation problems that are more difficult than the typical valuation where we face a choice among goods and services which are at least in some senses substitutes for one another and whose supply can be increased if we wish. Thus economists, operating on work-a-day problems, do not regularly face the "ultimate value" questions which people often have in mind when they say that "air" or "life" or the "natural environment" have incalculable value. The economist would agree that the *total value* of each of these is infinite but would quickly add that total value is rarely a relevant concept. What is usually relevant in decision making is *marginal value*, the value of small changes in the quality and quantity of each of these. It is this focus on the margin where decisions are made that moves economics away from the larger "philosophic" questions.

4. ECONOMICS AS THE SCIENCE OF VALUE AND CHOICE

Economics received its current "modern" definition from Lionel Robbins in his 1935 book, An Essay on the Nature and Significance of Economic Science, where he defined economics as "the science which studies human behavior as a relationship between ends and scarce means which have alternative uses." Note how broadly Robbins has cast the economist's net. Any problem which involves the pursuit of specifiable, multiple-objectives for which the means available are scarce and usuable for the pursuit of more than one objective is an economic problem. Clearly in that sense the use of the resources of the social and physical environment and the services flowing from them which we have labeled the QOL is an economic problem and behavior with respect to them can be subjected to

---

*Ibid, pp. 45-46.

economic analysis. One thing the study of that behavior can
tell us is how individuals *value* the goods and services which
flow from these environments as compared to the goods and services they can obtain from manufacturing and service activity.
The private human made environment of the home, yard, restaurant, and theater provide services to individuals as does the
social and natural environment. The economic analysis we have
tried to carry out has asked what human behavior in pursuit of
each of these types of environments tells us about the relative valuations individuals have made.

It is important to note that economics focuses not on the
internal psychological state of the individual but on the external environment, the social and material condition which
influence that internal state. Thus the QOL as we have defined it is not the state of mind or psychic condition or degree
of happiness which an individual attains but the external cir-
cumstances which allow the satisfaction of those needs and desires. One can attain happiness by either controlling or li-
miting needs and desires or by obtaining access to the external material and social resources which satisfy them. "Budd-
hist" economics would emphasize the former. Conventional economics emphasizes the latter. By taking for granted, taking
"as given," the tastes and preferences of individuals, conventional economics avoids the philosophic and social-psychologi-
cal problems most people associate with the study of "value"
but in the process grossly oversimplifies the analysis of human behavior. We will discuss this limitation more fully below. Our point here is to make explicit exactly what the economist is focusing on when studying the "value of the quality
of life."

The quality of life is productively open to economic analysis because it is in fact pursued by individuals. Such ac-
tive pursuit indicates that high quality natural and social
environments are scarce. They are not available in unlimited
supply. That is what makes the quality of life, at the margin, valuable. If high quality environments were available at
no effort to everyone, no value would be attached to one environment compared to another. As a result of the scarcity
and value of high quality environments, people commit scarce,
valuable resources to their pursuit. They change their behavior and trade-off one desirable objective for another as they
use their resources to improve their condition. It is this
use of resources which have alternative uses in the pursuit of
a particular objective that gives the QOL an economic aspect.
If the "resources" commited to the pursuit of an objective are
solely "inner" resources, for instance thought, care, psychic
energy, etc., one could safely argue that we were outside the
realm of "economic goods" or "economic objectives" or "economic resources." The pursuit of love or respect using only
one's inner resources would certainly fall into this category.
But even here the economic way of thinking about a problem in

terms of relative values and trade-offs may be useful in rationally commiting scarce inner resources to the pursuit of
conflicting objectives.

It is when the scarce resources used in the pursuit of an
objective are not just personal "inner" resources but "external" resources which have valuable alternative uses to significant numbers of other people that the problem becomes clearly economic. Although there is an important broad gray area
here which centers on human productivity in work, where personal "inner" resources are crucial, the natural and social
environments clearly represent "external" resources which are
valuable for a variety of conflicting uses to significant numbers of people and therefore are economic resources the pursuit of which are subject to economic analysis.

The role of economics in this regard is to establish the
relative value of the goods and services the social and natural environment can provide so that rational decisions about
the use of those resources can be made. In this limited sense,
economics is a science of value and choice. Other analytical
approaches, philosophy, psychology, sociology, and cultural
anthropology, certainly are also useful in analyzing the "value of the quality of life." Whether economics has something
of special importance to offer relative to these other approaches is a matter of judgement. Given that economics has
only recently turned its attention to this area, the analytical tools currently available are usually crude and the data
base almost non-existent. Thus, it may be too early to judge
the contribution economics can make. The point we are trying
to make here is that economics does have *something* to contribute and given the importance of what is at stake it would be
foolish to ignore that contribution.

5. THE LIMITS OF CONVENTIONAL ECONOMIC ANALYSIS

Scattered throughout the above discussion are comments
which suggest that economics as it is now formulated and prac-
ticed, although useful in analyzing the use of environmental
resources, has serious limits and biases. We now try to draw
these critical concerns together.

A. The Assumption of Independent, Atomistic Economic Actors

One of the basic assumptions in conventional economics is
that economic actors can engage in production or consumption
without having effects on one another which cannot be mediated
by private contractual arrangements. With this assumption, it
was easy to "prove" that a market economy and private ownership of resources leads to the best of all possible resource
allocations. Clearly this assumption, whatever its scientific status, had great ideological importance for it supported
a political philosophy of extremely limited public interven-

tion in economic affairs. It was the foundation of the theory
of a private enterprise economy.

In recent years there has been a substantial shift away
from that assumption by economists who have found in "externalities" and "public goods" significant examples of "market
failure." It has become clear that in an urban industrialized
society, not only are we as economic actors interdependent, not
independent, in our consumption and production activities, but
also the contractual arrangements to take into account *all* of
the important interdependencies would be so costly and admin-
istratively difficult as to be impossible. If these interdependencies which the market cannot rationalize are pervasive,
as some including the present writer would argue, significant
and broad ranging social interventions may be necessary.

B. The Assumption of Static, Exogenous Preferences

The interdependence discussed above applies not only to
production and consumption activities which have "spill-over"
or "neighborhood effects" such as the familiar air, water, and
noise pollution examples as well as problems of congestion and
rapid depletion of non-renewable resources. That interdependence also affects the preferences and tastes individuals have
as well as their feelings of well being.

Economists can make the case for the importance of virtually unlimited commodity production only because they ignore
a basic interdependency in "need" formation. Conventional economic theory assumes that individual wants originate with the
individual and are virtually unlimited in the aggregate. From
that they conclude that the more commodities that are made a-
vailable to the individual, the more wants are satisfied, and
thus, the higher will be the individual's level of well being.

The problem is that, as Thorstein Veblen pointed out long
ago, peoples' wants are interdependent and social in origin.
Your consumption of a good may lead me to want to consume it
even though I had had no such desire or "want" before. Thus
your consumption makes me feel worse off than I would have if
you had not through your consumption triggered that response
in me. My consumption of that good will *not* make me better
off than I had been initially; it will simply bring back to
the point of satisfaction at which I was originally. My purchase attempts to *maintain* my well being at a particular level. It is a *cost* of maintenance *not* a *benefit* in the sense
of an addition to my well being. To the extent that individuals judge their well being in relative terms, relative to
their peers or relative to their social superiors or inferi-
ors, additional commodity production may be no more success-
ful at improving welfare than arms expenditures in the context of an arms race adds to the military security of any
party. Similar things can be said about the mutual interaction that brings about taste formation and especially about

the role of advertising.

Given that economists tend to ignore these interdependencies, there are sound reasons to doubt their conclusions about whether a particular use of resources will in fact add to the population's welfare or well being. Until these Veblenesque relationships are taken into account, little that is reliable can be said by economists about individual or collective aggregate well being.

The increased emphasis by economists on "externalities," "public goods" and "market failure" may not be due simply to the increased interdependency which characterizes a modern industrial society. As the production of commodities for private consumption has grown, the value of such additional production may have declined relative to the value of collectively used amenity resources. In a Maslowvian sense, the satisfaction of basic material needs has given priority to a new set of social and aesthetic needs. We have moved up a step in the Maslowvian hierarchy of needs. These new needs are not as easily satisfied by private individual action through the consumption of commodities, and so we have turned to social or collective action to fulfill them. This reference to Maslow's hierarchy of needs points to another limitation of conventional economic analysis.

C. Needs vs Wants as the Reference Point
    in the Analysis of Human Choice*

Conventional economics assumes an extremely primitive psychological model of human beings, a model with which even the most fundamentalist behavioral psychologist would be uncomfortable. Economists have largely avoided dealing with psychology at all by assuming that an individual's or a society's "tastes and preferences" are set as a result of unexplored forces and remain fixed for the period of analysis. Thus they can be taken as given and exogenous to the economic activity being analyzed. Those "tastes and preferences" are looked upon as a set of *wants* which when satisfied make homogeneous contributions to welfare which differ from one another only in the quantitative degree or size of the satisfaction obtained. Thus "satisfaction" or "welfare" can be looked upon as a single dimensioned concept. Earlier in the history of economic thought, this *one* purpose, *the* single goal in life, was labeled "utility." Contemporary economists have tried to avoid the embarrassment such a primitive assumption would cause by verbally abandoning the concept. But their formal analysis does involve maximizing a single dimensioned quantity

---

*For a very readable account of the importance of this point, see The Challenge of Humanistic Economics, Mark A. Lutz and Kenneth Lux, Benjamin/Cummings Publishing, 1979.

to which all human objectives can be reduced. It does not matter whether they explicitly claim that it is a measurable quantity of a psychic substance called utility which at some point a "hedonimeter" will be able to measure and record, as the early neoclassical economist assumed and our texts still suggest. Clearly the same basic assumption is still being made by economists.

Implicitly this Benthamesque "Utilitarian" approach recognizes only a single human need, the need to maximize utility. Within this context all needs are reducible to this primary one and the satisfaction of any one want can be substituted for or traded off against any other. Given the assumed single dimensioned nature of all human needs, the rational economic actor can be pictured as rationally calculating the quantitatively maximum utility position by mentally shifting expenditures of limited time, money, and emotional resources among the available potential sources of satisfaction. The mathematical tools of differential calculus and functional analysis are readily applicable to the modeling of this type of decision making.

The assumed *reducibility* of *needs* to one undifferentiated *want* has neither always been a part of economics nor has it gone unchallenged. Karl Menger, one of the co-founders of neoclassical economics in the late 19th century, presented his explanation of diminishing marginal utility in terms of a *hierarchy* of needs.* As one need became satisfied, its importance declined and a new need became dominant. All needs were not the same. Some dominated others. Contemporary mathematical economist Nicholas Georgescu-Roegen has been criticizing the assumption of the reducibility of wants to a single maxim and for three decades.** More recently the work of psychologist Abraham Maslow has been applied to economic theory to develop a "humanistic" school of economics which specifically rejects the use of "wants" in favor of a hierarchy of irreducible needs.***

If needs are not reducible to a generalized want and human beings are motivated by a hierarchically oriented set of irreducible needs which are satisfied in sequential order, several serious problems develop for economists. First, needs become dynamic. They are changed by the very process of sat-

---

*Karl Menger, Principles of Economics, Glencoe, Illinois, The Free Press, 1950.

**See "The Pure Theory of Consumer's Behavior," Quarterly Journal of Economics, 1936, pp. 545-93, "Choice, Expectation and Measurability," Quarterly Journal of Economics, 68, 4, (November 1954), pp. 503-534 and "Vilfredo Pareto and His Theory of Ophelimity" in Energy and Economic Myths, New York; Pergammon Press, 1976, Chapter 13.

***See Lutz and Lux, op. cit.

isfying them. They are not static or "given" by some outside
force. People individually and collectively by their very
economic activity change, modify, and create new needs. This
problem was discussed above. Secondly, any given good or service may be satisfying several different irreducible needs simultaneously, each of those needs being ranked in a hierarchy
according to importance. In this situation it is impossible
to describe all choices individuals make in terms of opportunity costs or trade-offs. Some of the most basic tools of the
economist such as the indifference curves, marginal rates of
substitution, and marginal utility cease to be applicable.

The importance of this to our analysis is that implicitly
we may seem to have assumed that the quality of life has a
common dimension with all other human pursuits and that this
common dimension can be expressed in terms of a single quantitative measure, dollars. That is, our analysis may seem to
adopt the single need hypothesis on a grand crude scale: all
human values can be reduced to dollar terms. In addition, by
ignoring the dynamic nature of needs, we may be confusing actions tied to previous need priorities with actions tied to
the pursuit of more recently evolved needs in a very confusing
way. By assuming a fixed set of tastes and preferences we may
be misinterpreting historical and current data.

We have considerable sympathy with the above critique of
conventional economics' treatment of human needs. The impact
of this criticism on the legitimacy of our conclusions is,
however, unclear. If for significant portions of the population, the needs that could be satisfied by the purchase of
commodities on the commercial market for private use had been
satisfied to a degree sufficient to make the need for additional income a lower priority need in a hierarchy of needs and to
raise the pursuit of a higher quality living environment to
top priority, personal money income would no longer be a dominant motivating force in those peoples' lives. In that situation, individuals would focus on attaining the high quality
environment subject to some minimum income constraint. Money
income would not be considered a substitute for a quality environment. In the individuals' mind, money could not be
traded-off for a higher quality environment. Money would be
ignored in decision making about the choice of environments as
long as the minimum was attained. In that situation the money
income given up would not be a relevant measure of the value
of the QOL. Additional money income, being a lower priority
need in a hierarchy of irreducible needs, would have no relevant value in relation to environmental needs. This is not
simply to say that the "marginal utility" of income would have
fallen to zero or simply that the marginal rate of substitution had become zero. As a secondary or tertiary consideration, other things equal, or in comparison to other objectives
also of lower rank in the hierarchy, money income most likely
would be a relevant consideration. But in the choice at is-

sue, it would not and thus would be no more appropriate as a measure of the value of the QOL than would gallons of water or pounds of table salt. Money income measures in this hypothetical situation would simply be silly; they would convey no reliable or understandable information.

They would be silly, that is, unless what was at issue *was* the loss of income. And in environmental debates the loss of money income or jobs often *is* the issue. In this situation, where the relative importance of high quality environments and money income is at issue, the use of money income as the unit in which to measure the relative value of the QOL would seem to be quite appropriate. It shows that individuals *are* willing to give up money income for environmental amenities. The more they are in fact willing to give up, obviously the more important improvements in the QOL are *relative* to increases in money income. And that usually is one of the main points at issue. Thus the analysis used in this study would seem to be appropriate or at least relevant.

Further, it would seem that for much of the population, QOL and money income still are substitutes. For higher money incomes, a significant part of the population will accept significantly degraded work and living environments. In this situation, there is no question of the appropriateness of the use of a money income measure of value.

The problems created by the existence of a dynamic set of preferences were discussed in earlier chapters. Two points will be underlined here. If the population is in the process of moving from one need in the hierarchy (private commodity consumption) to another (higher quality physical and social environments), past priorities and behavior patterns will not be good indicators of present and future priorities. The relative value of "produced private commodities" would be expected over time to fall relative to "non-reproducible" natural environments and "social" environments. This shift in relative values over time should be considered in all policy decisions which have long run implications.

Second, to the extent individuals have invested time, energy, and other resources in developing the ability to enjoy a particular environment, degradation of that environment may well involve losses far in excess of those indicated by the decisions of the marginal migrant. These losses should not be ignored.

D. Qualitative *vs* Quantitative: The Economics of Quality

In our discussion of the "quality of life" we very quickly glossed over just what that "package" of environmental services we labeled the QOL contained. It in fact contains a varied mix of many different physical and social attributes which do not necessarily bear any determinant relationship to one another. Thus, between regions, the character of each service can vary independently of the others. The "difference in the quality of life" between two regions is an unspecified difference in the mix and character of the services. That unspecified mix and lack of a determinant relationship between the elements of the mix is what has led people to use the word "quality" when referring to these environmental services. It is not that one cannot quantitatively measure the elements of the mix. Air pollution, visual clarity, crime, congestion, community participation, mental health, etc. can be measured. In Chapter 5 we discussed the ways in which literally hundreds of quantitative variables were used to measure the QOL. The word "quality" is chosen not as an opposite of quantity but to describe the situation where a single dimension or a manageable number of controlable dimensions cannot be adequately used to characterize a resource or set of services or a product. Its varying "qualities" become important.

This is not an unusual situation. As Lancaster* has pointed out, commodities themselves are rarely what individuals seek. It is the *mix* of various services or attributes of which the commodity is the carrier which the individual seeks. A commodity is a "bundle" of qualities each of which has a different importance to the user. Thus "qualitative" concerns are fundamental even to the description of marketed commodity oriented behavior. This concern, then, is not something unique to the consideration of environmental services.

It is safe to say, however, that Lancaster's message about the importance of qualitative considerations in economics and the significant mathematical complications it adds to economic modeling of rational choice has been largely ignored by all but a few mathematically and theoretically oriented economists. If one adds to this multiple quality view of goods and services the irreducibility of hierarchically ordered wants, a significant additional complication is added. In combination they indicate the grossly inadequate view of the conventional economist's model of individuals systematically weighing the contribution each potential good and service could make to their utility as they seek to maximize that utility. This simplistic model of the human psyche and human choice has been held on to by economists because it allows a totally quantitative approach to choice, quantitative in the sense of a single relevant dimension, utility, which is adequate to completely describe the importance of the goods or services under consideration.

Abandoning this crude but mathematically simple model, does not mean abandoning mathematical analysis in economics. Both Lancaster and Georgesco-Roegen are mathematical economists. What is required is an abandonment of the mathematics

---

*Kelvin J. Lancaster, <u>Consumer Demand: A New Approach</u>, Columbia University Press, New York, 1971.

which economists rather slavishly borrowed from physics and which physics long ago abandoned, the differential calculus, functional analysis, and simultaneous equations, for the mathematics of set theory, lexicographic orderings, and simultaneous inequalities. Although mathematics remains an extremely important tool in economic analysis, the mathematics is of a sort which underlines the qualitative, non-mechanical character of rational choice. The basis is lost for the neoclassical economists' quantitatively oriented human psyche operating as a "hedonimeter" constantly calculating the potential additional "utils" of satisfaction from each possible choice. The new model of human choice presents a significantly more complicated and more complete picture. Unfortunately, very little undergraduate teaching makes use of the new model. The older "utility" oriented, one-dimensional model continues to dominate. This justifies criticism that economics is excessively "quantitative," "quantitative" in the sense of being one-dimensional and ignoring the crucial importance of qualitative considerations. Economics in this more primitive form can in fact be dangerous to human values and justifies Woodworth's warning that:

high Heaven
rejects the lore
of nicely calculated less or more.

Several generations of British economists have lived with that warning on the walls of King's College Chapel at Cambridge University. But it has yet to be taken seriously by the economics profession.

7
Economics, Economic Growth, and Economic Well-Being

1. INTRODUCTION

The previous Chapters have tried to look at what most people in past environmental debates have considered "non-economic" aspects of individual and social life from a strictly economic point of view. The argument has been that the QOL is as much a part of our economic welfare as anything else is or can be. In the process of developing that argument and trying to develop measures of the economic value of the QOL, some highly abstract theoretical and statistical analysis was necessary. The difficult, abstract nature, and tenuousness of some of that argument may have obscured the central hypotheses and tentative conclusion which have emerged. In this Chapter we draw together those hypotheses and conclusions and discuss their importance for the way we think about economic growth and economic well being. We will present these results as bold assertions intended to encourage more debate, discussion, theoretical analysis and empirical testing.

2. GENERAL CONCLUSIONS

A. In an Economy Where Resources, Especially Human Resources, Are Reasonably Mobile, No Area Can Be Substantially Better or Worse Off Than the Nation

The general theoretical conclusion of this paper is that because most areas are embedded in a national market economy which allows free labor mobility and because the work force is highly mobile, they, individually, on balance, cannot be substantially better or worse off than the rest of the nation when judged in terms of the total real income the population receives. Each can be different in the sense of offering residents a different mix of social characteristics, physical communities, cost of living, and money income, but it cannot be substantially superior or inferior. However, given that

individuals may have chosen to stay in a particular area or
locate there because of the particular mix of characteristics
or have invested in developing their ability to enjoy that mix
currently available, significant changes, even if accompanied
by rising money incomes, may well make them substantially
worse off. This is because many residents may value the a-
rea's particular mix of environmental resources more highly
than the marginal migrant to that area does. To them, the
differential value of the area's QOL relative to the nation is
higher than the wage differential suggests.

The work force *is* highly mobile. To use the example of
Montana as we have throughout this study, between 1965 and
1970, 175,000 people either moved into or moved out of Montana.* Fully 25 percent of the 1970 population was involved
in migration during a single five-year peiod. Between 1970
and 1976, almost one-third of the state's population was involved in migration to or from the state.** Similar patterns
would be found for any reasonably large geographic area in the
United States. With such population movements, disequilibria
in labor markets would be quickly eliminated.

Migration widely spreads the net benefits some areas enjoy and works towards eliminating the disadvantages others
have. However, as argued above, this does not mean that the
resulting distribution of population is in any sense socially
optimal. It is theoretically possible that national and state
social policies which both managed environmental change and
controlled migration could raise everyone's level of well being.

B.   An Area's Lower per Capita Income Is Not Necessarily
     a Sign of Lower Levels of Welfare

In particular, many semi-rural, small city regions' lower wages and money incomes are *not* a measure of a disadvantage
their residents suffer relative to the rest of the nation.
Mostly they are a measure of the *advantage* these residents enjoy in lower cost of living and higher quality of life and
compensate for that advantage in a way that leaves them with
approximately the same average real total income as available
elsewhere in the country.***

---

*Paul E. Polzin, "Montanans on the Move," Montana Business
Quarterly (Summer 1975):6.

**Social Security Administration, "Continuous Work History
Sample," Area 81 A, Montana.

***More accurately, the "last" migrants to choose to come to
an area or not to move from the area (the "marginal migrants")
are neither better off or worse off there than they would be
in other parts of the country. Intra-marginal people may be
better off where they are than that level of total real income which brings equilibrium to the national labor market.

That higher quality of life is associated with the smaller cities, semi-rural, and rural environments in which they
live as well as the higher quality natural physical environment they enjoy.

It would be very difficult, without this explanation, to
understand why, in the face of wages which are 5 to 35 percent
below those available elsewhere, not only do existing residents stay in these areas but, during the 1970s, residents of
"high income" large, urban industrial regions also moved into
these low-wage areas in sufficient volume to add, on net, to
these regions' populations.

C. Economic Growth and Growth in Economic
    Welfare May Not Be Closely Linked

Given the above results, one has to ask why assertions
about the "lagging" rural and small city economies and the
"need for more rapid economic growth" have dominated discus-
sions of the well being of these areas. The most convincing
answer to this question that we have found follows Molotch's
analysis.* Growth directly benefits the property interests of
a particular sector of the population: owners of local businesses, land investors, realtors, bankers, etc. These people
also make up the sector of the population which dominates
state and local political activity. They are *the* most important and "responsible" group in the population. Upon them
rests the funding of most political campaigns; they are, in
their daily business activities, regularly in contact with
state and local government; those governments' decisions directly affect their profits and profit-earning opportunities.
Even nominally independent and critical institutions such as
local newspapers and universities find their interests are
also tied to expansion and growth and financial support of
profitable businesses. In this situation, it is not surprising that the conventional economic "world view" or ideology
closely reflects the interests of this dominant, but minority,
sector of the population. It is not at all clear that the
rest of the population benefits from such growth to the same
degree or at all.

Several familiar arguments have tried to link growth and
the interests of the business community to the general interests of the population. These are very briefly discussed
below.

i. Rapid growth in a region creates jobs and reduces
unemployment. Rapid growth does not create jobs; it determines the spatial distribution of them within the national

---

*Harvey Molotch, "The City as a Growth Machine: Towards a Po-
litical Economy of Place," American Journal of Sociology, 82,
No. 2, pp. 309-332.

economy. With a mobile labor force one can expect the population to follow the jobs. Thus rapid growth will draw to an
area increasing numbers of migrants adding to the growth but
also providing competition for the available jobs. Thus local
unemployment may be unaffected or actually rise. Molotch, for
instance, shows that there is no correlation between the rate
of growth of an area and its unemployment rate.* Rapidly
growing areas often have unemployment rates above the national
average.

ii. Growth reduces the forced outmigration of a region's
young people and the accompanying social disruption, personal
pain, and loss of "human capital." This argument is probably
the emotionally most powerful argument for efforts to expand
the level of economic activity within a region. Unfortunately,
there is a substantial literature which challenges its basic
assumption, namely that outmigration is caused by economic
conditions in a particular area. Lowry** found that economic
conditions in a local area had no impact at all on outmigration. Demographic features, primarily the size of the youth-
ful cohort, the level of education, and the previous moving
patterns of the population, determined the rate of outmigration. Labor markets adjusted not through outmigration but
through economic conditions affecting the rate of *inmigration*.
Thus *net* migration rates (inmigration minus outmigration) do
adjust labor market supply to local labor demand (economic
conditions). More recently, Miller,*** Wrighton and Ga-
ton,**** and Morgan***** have developed and modified these results. They now must be stated as follows: Economic conditions have an extremely small but statistically measurable effect on outmigration but demographic variables are the dominate determinant of the rate of outmigration.
    This suggests that any area which has a relatively well-
educated and relatively large population of young people and
a total population dominated by individuals who moved from
some other state to live in that area will have a high rate of
outmigration no matter what happens to the local economy.
"The-grass-is-greener" mentality of the most mobile part of

---

*Ibid., pp. 321-325. Also see his references.

**Ira S. Lowry, Migration and Metropolitan Growth: Two
Analytical Models (Los Angeles: Institute of Government and
Public Affairs, University of California, 1966).

***Edward Miller, "Is Outmigration Affected by Economic Condi-
tions," Southern Economic Journal (January 1975): 396-405,
replies to the "Comments" listed in the following footnotes.

****Fred Wrighton and Paul Gatons, "Comment," SEJ (October
1974):311-313.
*****Celia Morgan, "Comment," SEJ (April 1976):752-758.

the population will not be much affected by local economic
conditions. Conventional economic growth-oriented policy,
if it were effective, would not significantly reduce outmigration. One final comment: to the extent birthrates continue to
fall towards a replacement rate, even ignoring the results
discussed here, natural population growth will no longer "require" a rapidly growing economy to provide jobs for all the
new young workers who wish them. However, the birth rate will
be above replacement levels well into the next century.

    iii. Economic growth helps to eliminate poverty. This
argument suggests that only upper-income groups can afford to
worry about the value of amenities and consider sacrificing
money income for those amenities. For low income groups money
income is of dominant importance and expansion of the economy
is the most likely way to boost the money income received by
low income residents.

    This argument must be challenged in several ways. First,
it is not at all clear that lower income residents of rural
and semi-rural areas hunt, fish, or make use of the natural
environment less than higher income residents. They may par-
ticipate more because it is a cheaper form of recreation. Low
income individuals may have a lower "willingness to pay" to
obtain access to these environmental resources, but this does
not mean that they are of lower value to these people. It is
only a sign that their income is low and they cannot afford to
pay more. Considerable numbers of rural as well as urban residents of America's "hinterland" live in "voluntary poverty"
in the pursuit of a particular way of life centered on the
natural environment.

    Secondly, as incomes rise over time, we may be able to
project that the tastes and preferences of low income individuals (if they differ from higher income individuals now) will
move in the direction of evaluating amenity values more highly. In long run economic policy, this sort of shift should be
taken into account.

    Third, and most important, economic growth is unlikely to
change the relative position of low income individuals. They,
compared to the national average, will remain "low income"
and significantly excluded from mainstream social and economic
activity. There is no evidence that economic growth changes
the relative distribution of income. Individuals who, because
of education discrimination, training, work history, cultural
background, physical or emotional handicap, etc., now have a
relative disadvantage in the labor market will, in the face of
competition from the inmigrants which economic growth brings,
fare no better and may fare worse.

D. The Disadvantages of Living in
   Small Cities and Rural Areas

Throughout this paper we have focused on the advantages
of living outside of the major urban and industrial concentra-
tions and have almost ignored the disadvantages: relative isolation, lack of access to a rich "cultural" life, lack of spe-
cialized services, distance from the "mainstream" of national
politics, cultural developments, entertainment, etc. We have
ignored these to emphasize a different point and focus on the
net advantages. It should be pointed out, however, that longer vacation times, rising incomes, and improvements in long
distance transportation (interstate highway system, air trans-
port, etc.), have significantly reduced the physical isolation
of the "hinterlands." Further, modern mass communication, in
particular cable color television as well as the simultaneous
release of first-run movies throughout the nation, have
brought into even the most isolated of Americans' homes much
of the nation's political and cultural life. This has further
reduced the "backwaters" aspect of living in small towns and
rural areas.

3. POLICY IMPLICATIONS

Here we simply list some of the tentative policy implications which flow from this paper. It must be emphasized that
the following assertions are based upon very preliminary ex-
ploratory work. They are offered as tentative warnings not as
firm guidelines.

A. The economic well being of the state relative to the nation, cannot be judged by the level of per capita money income
or similar narrowly defined economic indices. More broadly
defined socioeconomic indices need to be used and they must
take into account the valuable services which flow from the
social and physical environment.

Tentative steps in developing such statistical indicators
have been taken. The U.S. Environmental Protection Agency
sponsored a conference in 1972 which resulted in the volume,
*The Quality of Life Concept: A Potential New Tool for Decision
Makers.** EPA-funded research produced, in 1976, *Quality of
Life Indicators in U.S. Metropolitan Areas: A Comprehensive
Assessment.*** EPA has tried to start a regular statistical
series which will allow the monitoring over time of changes in

---

*EPA, Office of Research and Monitoring, Environmental Divi-
sion, 1973.

**Ben-Chieh Liu, EPA, Environmental Research Center. Also
published privately by Praeger Publishers with the subtitle,
"A Statistical Analysis."

various aspects of the QOL in different areas. Each state and city should consider doing the same so that it has some substantial context against which to judge the meaning of per capita income, employment, and migration statistics. Liu's indices of "individual economic well being," "environmental quality," "political health," "physical health," "education," "individual development," "individual equality," and "community living conditions" which were described in Table 5.13, Chapter 5 above, are interesting in that they try to deal more broadly with the social, political, and economic environment. Some serious analysis of such indices including an attempt to relate them to compensating wage differentials and migration patterns is in order. Some of the arbitrariness and bias which currently characterizes them is avoidable. A set designed specifically around each area's social and physical environment would both give us a broader feeling for trends and changes relative to the nation, and would point to data the absense of which currently limits our analysis.

Without some such broad-based socioeconomic indicators, the inevitable focus primarily on per capita income or other money income measures will continue to distort our view of the well being of an area's residents and the character of the area's economy.

B. Citizens in any particular area should be very careful about what is sacrificed in the pursuit of economic growth. To the extent that economic growth destroys parts of the physical and social environment which distinguishs the area and provides it with its higher QOL, the total real income of residents may be lowered even if money incomes rise. This study has focused on what, in the aggregate, these differential environmental advantages may be worth and has tried to show they are of substantial real value.

Knowing that the services supplied to an area by the natural and social environment are valuable and a significant part of their total real income is important. The quantitative value of these environmental services is also important information. Without this knowledge or understanding one is likely to be drawn to misleading or inaccurate conclusions about how well the area's economy is operating when the relatively low money incomes in rural areas and small cities are observed. However, for day-to-day policy decisions which affect the physical and social environment, knowledge of the total value of services flowing from those environments or the differential value relative to the rest of the nation is of little use. What is needed is knowledge of how a certain change in the environment will affect the value of the services flowing from the environment. It is this cost (or benefit) which has to be weighed against the benefits (or costs) associated with bringing about the modification. This study has focused on establishing the aggregate or total value. For

policy purposes one will need to know the incremental change
or marginal value.

Establishing this incremental value is a much more difficult problem than that addressed in this study. Here we only
outline the type of information which would be needed to deal
with it. First the relationship between the character of environment and the quantity and quality of the services flowing
from it needs to be established. For instance, how are fishing opportunities affected by water quality, stream flow, and
peak flows? This could be broken into two parts: how do these
physical factors affect the fish population and how do changes
in the fish population affect fishing opportunity and quality?
The final step would then be to establish how the citizens value the changes in the characteristics of fishing
brought on by the environmental change. In general, the analysis of any such environmental change can be broken down into
the technical problem of relating the physical environmental
changes to a change in the character of the services flowing
from that environment. After this technical relationship (the
production function) is established, one has to find how the
value of the services has changed (the demand function). This
latter is the more directly economic problem.

Each proposed change in the environment requires separate
study to determine both the technical production function and
the appropriate value or demand function. Air quality, major
industrial development of a particular type, roaded timber development, water diversions, or changes in water use, mining
activities, etc., each require separate analysis specific to
the area and population affected. No general results can be
put forth here except the historical warning that large dense
population centers and widespread industrial development have
in the past provided a very low QOL. This need for separate
individual analysis should not be taken to mean that the problem is hopeless. Economics in recent years has provided tools
which allow us to get at least some small handle on such non-
market evaluative problems. This, however, is beyond the
scope of the effort here although some rather crude attempts
in this direction were made in Chapter 5 when we tried to estimate the higher values associated with a particular area's
superior outdoor recreation opportunities, cleaner air, lower
crime rates and shorter travel times. But even in that analysis there was no analysis of how a change from the present
environment would affect these differential values. For this
much more detailed and specific analysis would be required.

C. Economic growth proposals should be analyzed to determine
the benefits they bring to existing residents and what the
distribution of those benefits is. Some or most existing residents may lose while business interests and recent immigrants gain. Rarely when a particular economic development is
discussed are the projected economic benefits broken down in

this way. The number of additional direct, indirect, and induced jobs are mentioned as is the total flow of additional
income. This is totally insufficient information for an a-
rea's residents to judge the real job and money income benefits of the development. The interaction of large scale development projects and population migration to the location
of the development needs to be studied as well as the interaction in the local job market of these inmigrants and the
existing local population. Without this sort of dynamic labor
market analysis, the distribution of the job benefits remains
indeterminant and the possibility that current residents do
not gain substantial new job opportunities remains. The same
is true for the indirect and induced income. To whom does
this flow: existing residents, new immigrants, workers, land-
lords, existing businesses, new businesses?

    Economic theory offers no obvious answers to these ques-
tions. It is *not* the case that we "know" that economic development benefits all or most of the current residents of an a-
rea. Without the above sort of analysis we can only guess.

D. The quality of life is heavily influenced by the size of
cities and the geographic distribution of population. This is
very difficult to control with currently available policy
tools, but relationships can be carefully studied and closely
monitored. Knowledge of how size and character of settlement
is related to environmental deterioration opens at least the
possibility of intervening ahead of time to change the relationship so as to minimize the damage.

E. An area or state cannot by itself increase the real income
of its population without restricting inmigration. If real
incomes increase in one area or the physical or social environment is improved, that area will face increased inmigration
which will put downward pressure on wages and increase the
strain on the social and physical environment. The overall
impact of such a set of changes cannot be predicted except
that it will change somewhat the total real income individuals
enjoy and at the margin that area will continue to provide a
total real income that is not much different from that available elsewhere in the economy although it may be different
from what it had previously been.

F. None of this is meant to suggest that an area's total real
income cannot change. Changes in a particular area which
cause a deterioration in the physical and social environment
which drew people to that area can lower some residents' total
real incomes while raising no one's. Likewise, nationwide
real money incomes may rise in ways which do not threaten environmental quality. This would raise total real income nationally and in most areas.

G. Given the fact that a particular area's economy is en-
meshed in a larger national economy in which market forces determine the flow of basic resources, it is very difficult for
state or local governments in the long run to develop or protect the economic well being of the population. A "private
enterprise" economy primarily allows private activities, co-
ordinated only by the market, to determine the overall level
of well being. Many social objectives of a collective nature
simply cannot be consciously pursued in a "private enterprise"
context. For state and local governments to be able to influence local economic well being, very strong policy measures
which directly influence the location of economic activity,
population, and capital are necessary.

Most states and cities have already taken steps in this
direction. The Major Facilities Siting Acts give local government agencies the power to decide where, if at all, any
large industrial operation is to be located within a state.
Public need and environmental compatibility are usually the
criteria upon which the decision is to be made. Through this
type of legislation state governments could become actively
involved in the determination of the location of economic activity. Similarly, county and city governments have turned to
land use planning to try to control the way in which rural a-
reas develop. County-wide plans attempt to specify ahead of
time the character of the economic activity which will be allowed to take place on each parcel of land. Location and density of population settlement as well as the location and
character of business activity could be controlled via these
tools. Major subdivisions, for instance, in most developed a-
reas must be shown to be in the "public interest" using a long
list of criteria.

Such legislation, however, may not actually actively involve the state and local government in economic location decisions. The government may primarily respond passively to
requests brought forth by the private sector, approving piecemeal all but the most environmentally destructive, and leaving
the initiative and primary decisions to the private sector.
In one major respect this is bound to be the case: it is far
easier for the government to refuse to allow a request to locate economic activity in a particular place than for the government to try to get economic activity with attractive characteristics to locate at a particular location within the
state. The government's effective tools are almost exclusively negative. Tax and subsidy schemes used by some states to
try to lure attractive businesses to particular areas primarily give away tax revenues to firms which because of market
forces would have located in the state anyway. Those market
forces are usually so strong that state tax policies are not a
determining consideration.

Finally, family migration decisions, one of the major
factors influencing population size and density and therefore

QOL, is not directly controlable by any government. Citizens
have a legal right to move freely across state boundaries in
the United States. No state can limit that right. The negative control of job opportunities could indirectly limit this
to a certain extent but only at some cost to existing residents, too. Land use planning could control density and location within the state to some extent. But the fundamental
primary decision is outside the control of state government.

Thus national market forces and legal considerations
severely constrain the public's ability to control or protect
its QOL. The tentative steps that state and local governments
have taken in this direction have faced significant political
opposition because they do limit "private enterprise." Further moves in this direction, however, are likely. The advantages and disadvantages of such additional policy measures
go beyond the scope of this paper, however.

We offer here only the warning that given the existence
of strong market forces and the legal and ideological con-
straints on the policy tools available to state and local government, indirect policy measures aimed at protecting an a-
rea's QOL may be costly and ineffective, or worse, counter-
productive. This may seem to be more of the negative and
"hopeless" prescriptions which earned economics the title of
the "dismal science." It is not meant in that way. The in-
tent is to underline the restrictions our current "political
economy" places on our ability to protect some of the most
valuable and important resources upon which we depend. We can
modify that socioeconomic system if we judge that the gains
outweigh the losses but well-intentioned "wishful" legislation is a frustrating and self-defeating way to go about that.
Bold, direct, and very controversial policy steps at the national and state level would be required.

H.   The above points underline the types of additional investigation into the relative economic value of the quality of
life in a particular area that is needed. This paper is bare-
ly a provocative beginning. If it is not followed up by more
rigorous research, of the sort outlined above, it will only
have added to the polemical debate without having settled any
of the important questions.

Appendix:
QOL Index Variables

On the following pages are lists of the variables the various analysts cited in Chapter 5 used in constructing their indices of well being or quality of life. In some cases, the weights attached to each variable are also given.

Table A1

VARIABLES USED TO COMPUTE LIU's STATE QOL INDEXES

(Used for Table 5.8)

I. Individual Status

  A. Existing Opportunity for Self-Support

    a. Labor force participation rate
    b. Percent of labor force employed
    c. Mean number of children under 18 years
    d. Cost adjusted mean family income per member
    e. Educational index

  B. Promote Maximum Development of Individual Capabilities

    a. Cost adjusted federal expenditures on education, manpower and training programs per capita
    b. Cost adjusted per capita local and state government expenditure on education
    c. Cost adjusted expenditure on vocational rehabilitation per case served
    d. Quality index of medical services
    e. Educational index

  C. Widen Opportunity for Individual Choice

    a. Mobility--motor vehicle registrations per 1,000 population
    b. Information

      1. Percent of total population subscribing to daily newspapers
      2. Commercial broadcast stations on the air per 100,000 population

    c. Equality index

II. Individual Equality

  A. Race and Sex Differences

    a. Race

      1. Ratio of nonwhite to white median family income adjusted for weeks (50-52) worked

2. Ratio of nonwhite to white male unemployment rate adjusted for education
3. Ratio of nonwhite to white female unemployment rate adjusted for education

b. Sex

1. Ratio of male to female unemployment rate adjusted for education
2. Ratio of male to female median income adjusted for education

B. Social-Economic Discrimination

a. Percent of Negro enrollment at public schools with 50-100% of Negro students
b. Percent of 7 to 13 year olds enrolled, nonwhite to white
c. Percent of males 16 to 64 years old with less than 15 years of school but some vocational training, nonwhite to white
d. Fair housing issue involved per 100,000 population
e. Number of black officials elected per 100,000 non-white population
f. Percent of urban households with income less than poverty level in renter occupied housing units, nonwhite to white

III. Living Conditions

A. General Conditions

a. Percent of families with income more than the poverty level
b. Weighted index of crime rate
c. Percent of occupied housing units with plumbing facilities
d. Cost adjusted cumulative comprehensive planning assistance grant for community planning per capita
e. Cost of living index

B. Facilities

a. State and local park and recreational areas, acres per 100,000 population
b. Number of beds in nursing and related care homes per 1,000 population
c. Hospital beds per 1,000,000 population
d. Number of telephones per 100 population

e. Library

1. Number of public libraries per 100,000 population
2. Library books per capita

f. Symphony orchestras per 100,000 population

C. Social and Environmental Conditions

a. Accident death rate per 100,000 population
b. Motor vehicle traffic mileage death rate by place
of accident, deaths per 100,000,000 vehicles miles
c. Marriage-divorce rate
d. Normal per year average of possible sunshine days
e. Average annual relative humidity
f. Health and welfare index

IV. Agriculture

A. Cost Adjusted Median Income of Farmers and Farm Mana-
gers
B. Average Value of Farm Marketing Per Farm
C. Percent of Farm Operators Reporting Less Than 49 Days
of Work Off Farm Annually
D. Number of Motor Trucks Including Pickups and Tractors
Other Than the Garden Tractors and Motor Tillers Per
Reporting Farm
E. Percent of Farm with Value Product Sold More Than
$100,000
F. Average Value of Land and Building Per Farm
G. Number of Tractors Per Farm

V. Technology

A. Promotion and Encouragement

a. Federal grants

1. Cost adjusted per capita federal obligations
to university and college for R & D
2. Cost adjusted per capita federal obligation to
university and college for academic science
3. Cost adjusted per capita federal obligations
to independent nonprofit research institutes
4. Cost adjusted per capita federal expenditures
on industrial R & D

b. Number of N.S.F. traineeships and fellowships a-
warded per 100,000 population

      c. Cost adjusted per capita industrial expenditures on R & D

B. Manpower: Number of Scientists Per 100,000 Population

VI. Economic Status

A. Cost Adjusted Personal Income Per Capita
B. Unemployment Rate
C. Manufacturing Industries

      a. Real value added per production worker
      b. Average weekly hours worked

D. Cost Adjusted Value of Construction Per Construction Employee
E. Per Capita Assets of Insured Commercial Banks
F. Educational Index
G. Technological Index
H. Agricultural Index

VII. Education

A. Percent of Males 16 to 21 Years Old Not High School Graduate
B. Percent of Persons 25 Years Old and Over Completed Median School Years Education
C. Ratio of Total Public Elementary and Secondary Enrollment to Population 5 to 17 Years Old
D. Public School Average Daily Attendance to Enrollment Ratio, 1968
E. Ratio of Higher Education Enrollment to Total Population 18 to 24 Years Old
F. Percent of Population 3 to 34 Years Old Enrolled
G. Percent of Selective Service Draftees Failed Mental Test
H. Ratio of High School Graduates to First Time College Students
I. Cost Adjusted Public School Expenditures to Personal Income Per Capita Ratio
J. Public School Pupil-Teacher Ratio

VIII. Health and Welfare

A. Medical Care

      a. Number of physicians per 100,000 population
      b. Number of dentists per 100,000 population
      c. Number of nurses per 100,000 population

d. Number of acceptable general hospital beds per 1,000,000 population
e. Average number of patients admitted per 1,000 population
f. Admission to state and county mental hospital per 1,000 population
g. Admission to public institutions for mentally retarded per 100,000 population
h. Nonwhite infant death rates
i. Death rates of heart diseases
j. Percent population served by fluorinated water supply
k. Price adjusted cost per day in hospital

B. Welfare

a. Number of lawyers per 100,000 population
b. Vocational rehabilitation served per 100,000 population
c. Cost adjusted average employer contribution rate of unemployment
d. Cost adjusted per capita state and local expenditure on public welfare
e. State and local expenditures on public welfare per $1,000 personal income
f. Cost adjusted average monthly benefits for retired workers
g. Cost adjusted public assistance per recipient to

1. Old age
2. Family with dependent children
3. Living veteran
4. Deceased veteran

h. Cost adjusted child welfare services expenditures per recipient

IX. State and Local Governments

A. Informed Citizenry

a. Percent of total population subscribing to daily newspapers
b. Commercial broadcast stations on the air per 100,000 population
c. Percent of voting age population registered
d. Percent of total registered population who voted in 1968 presidential election
e. Median school years completed

B. Professionalism of Administration

    a. Cost adjusted median salary of full-time employee
    b. Full-time government employment per 100,000 population
    c. Coverage of full-time employee by contributory system

        1. Retirement protection
        2. Health, hospital and disability
        3. Life insurance

    d. Percent of teachers with salary $9,500 and over

C. Performance of Administration

    a. Percent of general revenues from federal grants
    b. Cost adjusted per capita general revenues from federal grants
    c. Cost adjusted general revenues from own sources per $1,000 personal income
    d. Cost adjusted individual income tax revenues per capita
    e. Estimated market to assessed value locally assessed real property
    f. Weighted index of crime rate
    g. Selected employment service activities; total nonagricultural placement to nonagricultural job openings
    h. Educational index

Source: Ben C. Liu, "Variations of the Quality of Life in the United States by State, 1970," Review of Social Economy 32, no. 2 (October 1974).

Table A2

THE SPECIFIC STATISTICS USED IN CONSTRUCTION EACH
OF WILSON'S SOCIAL INDICATORS
(Used in Table 5.9)

I. The Status of the Individual

A. Enhance Individual Dignity Level to Public Assistance
for: (Average monthly payments)

Old-age assistance
Aid to families with dependent children
Social Security payments for: (average monthly payments)
Retired
Disabled
Living conditions index

B. Promote Maximum Development of Individual Capabilities
Quality of medical service index
Education Index

C. Widen Opportunities for Individual Choice

Equality index

II. Individual Equality

Eliminate Discrimination on the Basic of Race, Sex, and Religion

A. Current Economic Status

Ratio of nonwhite to white per capita median income adjusted for urban-rural differences in population distribution

Ratio of nonwhite to white employment rates

B. Current Economic Discrimination

Ratio of nonwhite to white income adjusted for occupation differences

Ratio of nonwhite to white income adjusted for education differences

C. Socio-economic Impairment Discrimination

Educational attainment as measured by the ratio of the white to nonwhite high school dropout rate

Educational attainment as measured by the ratio of nonwhite to white college graduate rate

Educational quality as measured by the ratio of white to nonwhite percent of draftees who failed the mental requirements portion of their pre-induction exams

Health

Ratio of white to nonwhite age adjusted mortality rates

Environmental conditions

Urban housing density as measured by the ratio of white to nonwhite percent of occupied units with 1.01 or more persons per room

Quality of urban housing as measured by the ratio of nonwhite to white percent of occupied housing units which are sound and have all plumbing facilities

Segregation of urban housing as measured by a weighted index of the extent of segregation by census block

III. Education

A. Output

One minus the high school dropout rate

Percent passing pre-induction Army mental examination

Percent of population ages 5-20 enrolled in high school

First-time college enrollees as a percent of high school graduates

Percent of population ages 18-44 enrolled in higher education

First-time professional and graduate students as a percent of full-time undergraduates

IV. Economic Growth

A. Output

Percentage increase in personal income, 1960-65

Percentage increase in per capita personal income, 1960-65

B. Input

Per capita capital outlay by state and local governments

Unemployment rate

Living conditions index

Technological change index

Education index

V. Technological Change

A. Promotion and Encouragement of Technological Change

Patents issued to residents of each state

Current expenditure on research in universities and colleges

Industrial research and development expenditures

Manpower

Number of scientists

NASA research contracts with universities and nonprofit organizations net sub-contracts

Military prime contracts for research

AEC research contracts with universities and nonprofit organizations

B. Education and Retraining

Enrollment in vocational and technical education as percent of population

Per capita expenditure for vocational education

VI.   Agriculture

    A.   Farm Level-of-Living Index

        Average value of land and buildings per farm

        Average value of sales per farm

        Percent of farms with telephone

        Percent of farms with freezer

        Percent of farms with automobiles

VII. Living Conditions

    A.   Remedy Slum and Poverty Conditions

        Total state technical assistance expenditure per poor person

        Economic opportunity assistance expenditure per poor person

        Percent of families with income under $3,000

        Percent of sound housing units with plumbing facilities

    B.   Reverse the Process of Decay in Larger Cities

        Per capita general expenditure of state and local governments for housing and urban renewal

        Weighted index of crime rates

    C.   Relieve the Necessity for Low-Income and Minority Groups to Concentrate in Central Cities

        Weighted index of median family income in central cities as a percent of SMSA median family income

    D.   Expand Parks and Recreation as Necessary to Meet Demand

        Per capita recreation area

VIII. Health and Welfare

    A. Medical Care

        Number of doctors per 100,000 population

        Number of dentists per 100,000 population

        Number of nurses per 100,000 population

        Number of acceptable general hospital beds per 1,000 population

        Number of acceptable mental hospital beds per 1,000 population

        Number of beds for long-term care for aged per 1,000 population

        Special and general patient days of care per 1,000 population

        Mental patient days of care per 1,000 population

        State and county mental hospital admissions per 100,000 population

        State and county mental hospital releases per 3,000 average daily patients

        Percent population served by fluorinated water supply

        Infant deaths per 1,000 live births

    B. Welfare

        Child health and welfare

        Child welfare expenditure per child under 21

        Mothers receiving medical clinic services

        Crippled children served

        Children receiving child welfare services

        Full-time caseworkers per 10,000 children

        Vocational rehabilitation

Rehabilitants per 100,000 population

Cases per counselor

Per capita expenditures

Public assistance

Old age assistance

Aid to families with dependent children

Source: Environmental Protection Agency, <u>The QOL Concept</u>, <u>op. cit.</u>

Table A3

VARIABLES USED IN SMITH'S INDICES OF SOCIAL WELL BEING
(Used in Table 5.10)

Criteria and Variables	Direction
I. INCOME, WEALTH AND EMPLOYMENT	
i. Income and Wealth	
1. Per capita annual income ($) 1968	+
2. Families with annual income less the $3000 (%) 1959	-
3. Total bank deposits per capita ($) 1968	+
ii. Employment Status	
4. Public assistance recipients (% population) 1964	-
5. Union members per 1000 non-agricultural employees 1966	+
6. White-collar employees (% of total) 1960	+
iii. Income Supplements	
7. Average monthly benefit for retired workers ($) 1968	+
8. Average monthly AFDC payments per family ($) 1968	+
9. Average monthly aid to the disabled ($) 1968	+
10. Average monthly old age assistance ($) 1968	+
11. Average weekly state unemployment benefit ($) 1968	+
II. THE ENVIRONMENT	
i. Housing	
12. Median value of owner occupied houses ($) 1960	+
13. Houses dilapidated or lacking complete plumbing (%) 1960	-

Criteria and Variables	Direc- tion

14. Index of home equipment (max.= 600) 1960   +

III. HEALTH

i. Physical Health

15. Households with poor diets (%) 1965   -
16. Infant deaths per 10,000 live births 1967   -
17. Tuberculosis deaths per million population 1967   -
18. Hospital expenses per patient day ($) 1965   +

ii. Access to Medical Care

19. Hospital beds per 10,000 population 1967   +
20. Physicians per 10,000 population 1967   +
21. Dentists per 10,000 population 1967   +
22. Persons covered by hospital health insurance (%) 1965   +

iii. Mental Health

23. Residents in mental hospitals etc. per 100,000 population, 1966   -
24. Patient days in mental hospitals per 1,000 population 1965   -
25. Mental hospital expenditures per patient day ($) 1965   +

IV. EDUCATION

i. Achievement

26. Illiterates per 1000 population 1960   -
27. Draftees failing armed service mental test (%) 1968   -

Criteria and Variables	Direc-tion

ii. Duration

    28. Median school years completed (x10) 1960   +

    29. Persons attended college per 1000 population aged 25 or over, 1960   +

iii. Level of Service

    30. Pupils per teacher 1968   -

    31. Public school expenditures per pupil ($) 1967   +

V. SOCIAL DISORGANIZATION

i. Personal Pathologies

    32. Alcoholics per 10,000 adults, 1970   -

    33. Narcotics addicts per 10,000 population 1970   -

    34. Gonorrhea cases per 100,000 population 1970   -

    35. Syphilis cases per million population 1970   -

    36. Suicides per million population 1967   -

ii. Family Breakdown

    37. Divorces 1966 per 1000 marriages 1968   -

    38. Husband and wife households (% of total) 1966   +

iii. Crime and Safety

    39. Crimes of violence per 100,000 population 1969   -

    40. Crimes against property per 10,000 population 1969   -

    41. Motor vehicle accident deaths per million population 1967   -

Criteria and Variables	Direc- tion

VI. ALIENATION AND PARTICIPATION

i. Democractic Participation

42. Eligible voters voting (%) 1964   –
43. Registered voters per 100 population of voting age 1968   +

ii. Criminal Justice

44. Jail inmates not convicted (%)
1970   –
45. Population per lawyer 1966   –

iii. Racial Segregation

46. Negroes in schools at least 95%
Negro 1968   –
47. City residential segregation index
(max. = 100) 1960   –

Source: David M. Smith, The Geography of Social Well Being in
the U.S., New York, McGraw-Hill, 1973, pp. 82-83.

Table A4

WEIGHTS USED IN SMITH'S PRINCIPAL COMPONENT ANALYSIS

(Used in Table 5.11)

COMPONENT 1:   GENERAL SOCIO-ECONOMIC WELL BEING (explained
               variance: 38.56%)
  highest loadings: -.9398 families with income less than $3000
                      -.9083 houses dilapidated etc.
                       .8951 benefits for retired workers
                       .8853 per capita income
                       .8651 dentists/10,000 population
                       .8556 AFDC payments
                       .8086 state unemployment benefit
                       .8065 value of owner-occupied houses
                      -.7993 households with poor diets
                      -.7993 infant deaths
                       .7868 public school expenditures
                      -.7834 mental test failures
                       .7780 eligible voters voting
                       .7749 white-collar employees
                       .7615 physicians/10,000 population
                       .7587 median school years completed

COMPONENT 2:   SOCIAL PATHOLOGY (explained variance: 13.74%)

  highest loadings: .8384 crimes of violence
                       .7236 syphilis cases
                       .6719 gonorrhea cases
                       .6528 narcotics addicts
                       .6422 school segregation
                      -.6325 registered voters
                       .6043 crimes against property
                       .5517 illiteracy
                       .5413 tuberculosis deaths
                      -.5329 index of home equipment

COMPONENT 3: MENTAL HEALTH (explained variance: 11.98%)

  highest loadings: -.8174 patient days in mental hospitals
                       .7999 hospital expenses/patient day
                      -.7940 residents in mental hospitals etc.
                      -.7800 hospital beds/10,000 population
                       .6323 divorces
                       .5583 suicides
                       .4932 mental hospital expenditures/patient
                             days
                       .4696 motor vehicle accident deaths

highest loadings: .4601 crimes against property
.4568 median school years completed
.4548 persons attended college

Source: David M. Smith, The Geography of Social Well Being in the U.S., New York, McGraw-Hill, 1973, p. 94.

Table A5

DATA USED BY LIU IN CONSTRUCTING QOL INDICES
(Used in Table 5.12)

Section 1.   Factors in Economic Component

Factor Effect and Weight		Factors
	I.	Individual Economic Well-Being
+ (.25)	A.	Personal income per capita ($)
	B.	Wealth
+ (.05)	1.	Savings per capita ($)
+ (.05)	2.	Ratio of total property income to total personal income
+ (.05)	3.	Percent of owner-occupied housing units
+ (.05)	4.	Percent of households with one or more automobiles
+ (.05)	5.	Median value, owner-occupied, single family housing units ($1,000)
	II.	Community Economic Health
+ (.07)	A.	Percent of families with income above poverty level
- (.07)	B.	Degree of economic concentration, absolute value
	C.	Productivity
+ (.014)	1.	Value added per worker in manufacturing ($1,000)
+ (.014)	2.	Values of construction per worker ($1,000)
+ (.014)	3.	Sales per employee in retail trade ($1,000)
+ (.014)	4.	Sales per employee in wholesale trade ($1,000)
+ 9.014)	5.	Sales per employee in selected services ($1,000)
+ (.07)	D.	Total bank deposits per capita ($)
	E.	Income inequality index
- (.035)	1.	Central city and suburban income distribution
- (.035)	2.	Percent of families with incomes below poverty level or greater

Factor Effect and Weight	Factors
	than $15,000
- (.07)	F. Unemployment rate
+ (.07)	G. Number of full-time Chamber of Commerce employees per 100,000 population

Section 2. Factors in Political Component

Factor Effect and Weight	Factors
	I. Individual Activities
	A. Informed citizenry
+ (.083)	1. Local Sunday newspaper circulation per 1,000 population
+ (.083)	2. Percent of occupied housing units with TV available
+ (.083)	3. Local radio stations per 1,000 population
+ (.25)	B. Political activity participation-ratio of Presidential vote cast to voting age population
	II. Local Government Factors
	A. Professionalism
+ (.02)	1. Average monthly earnings of full-time teachers ($)
+ (.02)	2. Average monthly earnings of other full-time employees ($)
+ (.02)	3. Entrance salary of patrolmen ($)
+ (.02)	4. Entrance salary of firemen ($)
+ (.02)	5. Total municipal employment per 1,000 population
+ (.02)	6. Police protection employment per 1,000 population
+ (.02)	7. Fire protection employment per 1,000 population
+ (.02)	8. Insured unemployment rates under state, federal, and ex-servicemen's programs
	B. Performance
- (.03)	1. Violent crime rate per 100,000 population
- (.03)	2. Property crime rate per 100,000 population
+ (.03)	3. Local government revenue per capita

Factor Effect and Weight		Factors
+ (.03)	4.	Percent of revenue from federal government
+ (.03)	5.	Community health index
+ (.03)	6.	Community education index
	C.	Welfare assistance
+ (.053)	1.	Per capita local government expenditures on public welfare ($)
+ (.053)	2.	Average monthly retiree benefits ($)
+ (.053)	3.	Average monthly payments to families with dependent children ($)

Section 3. Factors in Environmental Component

Factor Effect and Weight		Factors
	I.	Individual and Institutional Environment
	A.	Air pollution index
- (.05)	1.	Mean level for total suspended particulates ($\mu g/m^3$)
- (.05)	2.	Mean level for sulfur dioxide ($\mu g/m^3$)
	B.	Visual pollution
- (.033)	1.	Mean annual inversion frequency
- (.033)	2.	Percent of housing units dilapidated
+ (.033)	3.	Acres of parks and recreational areas per 1,000 population
	C.	Noise
- (.033)	1.	Population density in the central city of the SMSA, persons per square mile
- (.033)	2.	Motor vehicle registrations per 1,000 population
- (.033)	3.	Motorcycle registrations per 1,000 population
- (.10)	D.	Tons of solid waste generated by manufacturing per million dollars value added
- (.10)	E.	Water Pollution index
	II.	Natural Environment
	A.	Climatological data

Factor Effect and Weight	Factors
- (.05)	1. Mean annual inversion frequency
+ (.05)	2. Possible annual sunshine days
- (.05)	3. Number of days with thunderstorms occurring
- (.05)	4. Number of days with temperature of 90° and above
- (.05)	5. Number of days with temperatures of 32° and below

B. Recreation areas and facilities

+ (.125)	1. Acres of parks and recreational areas per 1,000 population
+ (.125)	2. Miles of trails per 100,000 population

Section 4. Factors in Health and Education Component

Factor Effect and Weight	Factors

I. Individual Conditions

A. Health

- (.125)	1. Infant mortality rate per 1,000 live births
- (.125)	2. Death rate per 1,000 population

B. Education

+ (.063)	1. Median school years completed by persons 25 years old and over
+ (.063)	2. Percent of persons 25 years and over, who completed 4 years of high school or more
- (.063)	3. Percent of males ages 16 to 21 who are not high school graduates
+ (.063)	4. Percent of population ages 3 to 34 enrolled in schools

II. Community Conditions

A. Medical care availability and accessibility

+ (.05)	1. Number of dentists per 100,000 population
+ (.05)	2. Number of hospital beds per 100,000 population
+ (.05)	3. Hospital occupancy rates
+ (.05)	4. Number of physicians per 100,000 population
+ (.05)	5. Per capita local government expenditures on health

Factor Effect and Weight	Factors
	B. Educational attainment
+ (.125)	1. Per capita local government expenditures on education
+ (.125)	2. Percent of persons 25 years old and over who completed 4 years of college or more

Section 5. Factors in Social Component

Factor Effect and Weight	Factors
	I. Individual Development
	A. Existing opportunity for self-support
+ (.018)	1. Labor force participation rate
+ (.018)	2. Percent of labor force employed
+ (.018)	3. Mean income per family member ($)
+ (.018)	4. Percent of children under 18 years living with both parents
- (.018)	5. Percent of married couples without own household
+ (.018)	6. Individual education index
	B. Promoting maximum development of individual capabilities
+ (.028)	1. Per capita local government expenditures on education ($)
+ (.028)	2. Percent of persons 25 years old and over who completed 4 years of high school or more
	3. Persons ages 16 to 64 with less than 15 years of school but with vocational training
+ (.014)	a. Percent of males
+ (.014)	b. Percent of females
+ (.028)	4. Individual health index
	C. Widening opportunity for individual choice
	1. Mobility
+ (.007)	a. Motor vehicle registration per 1,000 population
+ (.007)	b. Motorcycle registrations per 1,000 population
+ (.007)	c. Percent of households with one or more automobiles

Factor Effect and Weight		Factors
		2. Information
+	(.007)	a. Local Sunday newspaper circulation per 1,000 population
+	(.007)	b. Percent of occupied housing units with TV available
+	(.007)	c. Local radio stations per 1,000 population
		3. Spatial extension
-	(.011)	a. Population density in SMSA, persons per square mile
-	(.011)	b. Percent of population under 5 and 65+ living in central city
+	(.022)	4. Individual equality index
+	(.022)	5. Individual and institutional environment index

II. Individual Equality

A. Race

+	(.028)	1. Ratio of Negro to total persons median family income adjusted for education
+	(.028)	2. Ratio of Negro to total persons in professional employment adjusted for education
-	(.028)	3. Ratio of Negro males to total males unemployment rate adjusted for education, absolute value
-	(.028)	4. Ratio of Negro females to total females unemployment rate adjusted for education, absolute value

B. Sex

-	(.055)	1. Ratio of male to female unemployment rate adjusted for education, absolute value
-	(.055)	2. Ratio of male to female professional employment adjusted for education, absolute value

C. Spatial

-	(.037)	1. Percent working outside county of residence
-	(.037)	2. Income inequality index--central city and suburban income distribution, absolute value

Factor Effect and Weight		Factors
-	(.037)	3. Housing segregation index, absolute value
		III. Community Living Conditions
		A. General conditions
+	(.016)	1. Percent of families with income above poverty level
+	(.016)	2. Percent of occupied housing units with plumbing facilities
-	(.016)	3. Percent of occupied housing units with 1.01 or more persons per room
+	(.016)	4. Percent of occupied housing units with a telephone available
+	(.016)	5. Percent of workers who use public transportation to work
-	(.016)	6. Total crime rate per 100,000 population
-	(.016)	7. Cost of living index
		B. Facilities
		1. Recreational facilities
+	(.005)	a. Number of swimming pools per 100,000 population
+	(.005)	b. Number of camping sites per 100,000 population
+	(.005)	c. Number of tennis courts per 100,000 population
+	(.005)	d. Miles of trails per 100,000 population
+	(.018)	2. Number of banks and savings and loan associations per 1,000 population
+	(.018)	3. Number of retail trade establishments per 1,000 population
+	(.018)	4. Number of selected service establishments per 1,000 population
+	(.018)	5. Number of hospital beds per 100,000 population
+	(.018)	6. Volumes of books in the main public library per 1,000 population
		C. Other social conditions
-	(.018)	1. Death rate per 1,000 population
-	(.018)	2. Birth rate per 1,000 population
+	(.018)	3. Sports events in the metropolitan area

Factor Effect and Weight	Factors
	4. Cultural events in the metropolitan area
+ (.007)	a. Dance, drama, and music events
+ (.007)	b. Cultural institutions
+ (.007)	c. Fairs and festivals held
+ (.018)	5. Community health and education index
+ (.018)	6. Natural environment index

Source: B.C. Liu, _Quality of Life Indicators in U.S. Metropolitan Areas, 1970_, op. cit., Chapter 7.

Bibliography

Baier, Kurt and Rescher, Nicholas, eds., Values and the Fut-
    ure, The Free Press, New York, 1969, p. 40.
Baumol, William J. and Bowen, William G., Performing Arts: The
    Economic Dilemma, Twentieth Century Fund, New York, 1966.
Beesley, M.E., "The Value of Time Spent Travelling: New Evi-
    dence," Economica, May 1965.
Cebula, R.J., and Curran, Christopher, "Property Taxation and
    Human Migration," American Journal of Economics and Socio-
    logy, 37, No. 1 (Jan. 1978):43-49.
Cebula, R.J., and Vedder, Richard K., "A Note on Migration,
    Economic Opportunity, and the Quality of Life," Journal
    of Regional Science 13, No. 2 (1973):107-111, and Journal
    of Regional Science 16, No. 1 (April 1976):109-115.
Cournant, Paul N. and Rubinfeld, Daniel L., "On the Measure-
    ment of Benefits in An Urban Context: Some General Equili-
    brium Issues," Journal of Urban Economics, (July, 1978).
Fuchs, Victor, Differentials in Hourly Earnings by Region and
    City Size, 1959, Occasional Paper 101, Columbia University
    Press, 1961.
Gatons, Paul K. and Cebula, Richard J., "Wage Rate Analysis:
    Differentials and Indeterminancy," Industrial and Labor
    Relations Review 25, No. 2 (January 1972):202-212.
Georgescu-Roegen, Nicholas, "The Pure Theory of Consumer's Be-
    havior," Quarterly Journal of Economics, 1936, pp.545-593.
Georgescu-Roegen, Nicholas, "Choice, Expectation, and Measur-
    ability," Quarterly Journal of Economics, 68, 4, (Novem-
    ber 1954), pp.503-534.
Georgescu-Roegen, Nicholas, "Vilfredo Pareto and His Theory
    of Ophelimity," in Energy and Economic Myths, New York;
    Pergammon Press, 1976, Chapter 13.
Goldfarb, Robert S. and Yezer, Anthony M.J., "Evaluating Al-
    ternative Theories of Inter City and Interregional Wage
    Differentials, Journal of Regional Science 16, No. 3
    (December, 1976):353.

Hoch, Irving, "Variations in the Quality of Urban Life Among Cities and Regions," in Wingo and Evans, Public Economics and the Quality of Life, (John Hopkins, 1978).

Hoch, Irving, "Factors in Urban Crime," Journal of Urban Economics 1, No. 2 (April 1974):188, 204.

Hoch, Irving, "City Size Effects, Trends, and Policies," Science 193, September 3, 1976, p. 859.

Hoch, Irving, "Income and City Size," Urban Studies 9 (1972): 312.

Johnson, Paul R., "Labor Mobility: Some Costs and Returns," in Rural Poverty in the United States, a report by the President's National Advisory Commission on Rural Poverty (Washington: GPO), p. 247.

Kelley, Kevin C., "Urban Disamenities and the Measure of Economic Welfare," Journal of Urban Economics 4 (1977):379-388.

Lancaster, Kelvin, Consumer Demand: A New Approach, Columbia University Press, New York, 1971.

Lave, Lester B. and Seskin, Eugene P., Air Pollution and Human Health, Resources for the Future (Baltimore: John Hopkins University Press, 1977), Chapter 10.

Liu, Ben-Chieh, Quality of Life Indicators in U.S. Metropolitan Areas: A Statistical Analysis, Praeger Publishers, 1976.

Liu, Ben-Chieh, "Variations in the Quality of Life in the U.S. by State, 1970," Review of Social Economy 32, No. 2 (October 1974).

Liu, Ben-Chieh, "Differential Net Migration Rates and the Quality of Life," Review of Economics and Statistics, LVII, No. 3 (Aug. 1975):324-327.

Lowry, Ira S., Migration and Metropolitan Growth: Two Analytical Models (Los Angeles: Institute of Government and Public Affairs, University of California, 1966).

Lutz, Mark A. and Lux, Kenneth, The Challenge of Humanistic Economics, Benjamin/Cummings Publishing, 1979.

Menger, Karl, Principles of Economics, Glencoe, Illinois, The Free Press, 1950.

Meyer, John R. and Leone, Robert A., "The Urban Disamenity Revisited," in Wingo and Evans, Public Economics and the Quality of Life.

Michelson, I. and Tousin, B., "Comparative Methods of Studying the Costs of Controlling Air Pollution," Public Health Reports, Vol. 81, p. 505.

Miller, Edward, "Is Out-Migration Affected by Economic Conditions," Southern Economic Journal, (January 1975):396-405.

Molotch, Harvey, "The City as a Growth Machine: Towards a Political Economy of Place," American Journal of Sociology, 82, No. 2, pp. 309-332.

Morgan, Celia, "Comment," Southern Economic Journal (April 1976):752-758.

139

Morgan, James N., et al., Productive Americans (Ann Arbor:
    University of Michigan, Institute of Social Research,
    1966), Survey Research Monograph 43.
Moriarity, Barry M., "A Note on the Unexplained Residuals in
    North-South Wage Differential Models," Journal of Region-
    al Science 18, No. 1 (1978):105-108.
Nordhaus, W. and Tobin, J., "Economic Growth," NBER 50th Anni-
    versary Colloquium, Vol. V, Columbia University Press, New
    York, 1972.
Polinsky, A. Mitchell and Rubinfeld, Daniel L., "The Long Run
    Effects of a Residential Property Tax and Local Public
    Services," Journal of Urban Economics 5 (1978):241-262.
Polzin, Paul E., "Montanans on the Move," Montana Business
    Quarterly (Summer, 1975).
Polzin, Paul E., "State and Regional Wage Differentials,"
    Southern Economic Journal (January 1972):371-378.
Robbins, Lionel, An Essay on the Nature and Significance of
    Economic Science, Macmillan, London, 1935.
Seskin, Eugene, "Residential Choice and Air Pollution: A
    General Equilibrium Model," American Economic Review, 63
    No. 5 (December 1973):960-961.
Smith, David M., The Geography of Social Well-Being in the
    U.S., (New York, McGraw-Hill) 1973.
State of Montana, Air Quality Bureau, Department of Health,
    Annual Air Quality Data Summary for Montana, 1977.
State of Montana, Department of Fish and Game, Montana State-
    wide Outdoor Recreation Plan, 1969.
Thaler, R. and Rosen, S., "The Value of Saving a Life: Evid-
    ence from the Labor Market," in N. Terleckyj, ed., House-
    hold Production and Consumption, NBER, 1976.
Thurow, Lester C., "Psychic Income: Useful or Useless," Ameri-
    can Economic Review 68 (May 1978):142-148.
Tiebout, Charles M., "The Pure Theory of Local Government
    Expenditures," Journal of Political Economy, 64 (1956):
    416-424.
U.S. Bureau of Outdoor Recreation, Outdoor Recreation: A
    Legacy for America, 1973.
U.S. Environmental Protection Agency, Trends in the Quality of
    the Nation's Air, March 1977.
U.S. Environmental Protection Agency, The Quality of Life Con-
    cept: A Potential New Tool for Decision Makers, Office of
    Research and Monitoring, Environmental Studies Division,
    1973.
U.S., President's Commission on Law Enforcement and Administra-
    tion of Justice, Task Force Report: Crime and Its Impact
    (Washington, D.C., GPO, 1967), p. 28.
Vorhees, Alan M., et al., "Factors in Work-trip Lengths,"
    Highway Research Record, 14 (1966) 24-26.
Wertheimer, Richard F. II, The Monetary Rewards of Migration
    Within the U.S., The Urban Institute, Washington, 1970.

140

Wingo, Lowdon, "The Quality of Life: Toward a Micro-Economic Definition," Urban Studies 10 (1973):3.

Wingo, Lowdon and Evans, eds., Public Economics and the Quality of Life, Resources for the Future, (Johns Hopkins University Press, 1978).

Wrighton, Fred and Gatons, Paul, "Comment," Southern Economic Journal (October 1974) 311-313.

Index